# THE WORLD'S FASTEST CARS

**Publications International, Ltd.**

BY ALEX GABBARD • GRAHAM ROBSON
AND THE AUTO EDITORS OF CONSUMER GUIDE

## CREDITS

The editors gratefully acknowledge:

**Reg Abbiss**
Rolls-Royce Motor Cars, Inc.

**Martin Alfred**
L.A.T. Photographic Ltd.

**Kurt Antonius**
Acura Division, American Honda Motor Co., Inc.

**Jon Asher**
Asher Enterprises

*Auto Car* Magazine

**John Aycoth**
Edward Aycoth & Co.

**Ron Ballanti**
Joseph Molina P.R.

**Brad Bowling**
Saleen Autosport

**Bob Carlson**
Porsche Motorsport of North America

**Stefania Cohen**
Exclusive Motor Cars, Inc.
Upper Montclair, N.J.

**Mike Cook**
Jaguar Cars, Inc.

**Mirco Decet**

**Thomas Einkammerer**
Koenig Specials GmbH, West Germany

**Roland Flessner**

**Jim Follmer**
George Follmer Motorcars, Inc.
Montclair, Calif.

**Randy Fox**
Pontiac Motor Division, GM Corp.

**Mitch Frumkin**

**Alex Gabbard**

**Charles Giametta**

**Sam Griffith**

**Larry Gustin**
Buick Motor Division, GM Corp.

**David B. Hederich**
Chevrolet Motor Division, GM Corp.

**Deke Houlgate Enterprises**

**Steve Hurwitz**
Geltzer and Co., Inc.

**David S. Kaplan**
Callaway Engineering

**Tom Kowaleski**
Chrysler Motors

**Finlay MacDonald**
Rolls-Royce Motor Cars, Inc.

**Vince Manocchi**

**Ken McKay**
Ferrari North America

**Martha A. McKinley**
Porsche Cars of North America, Inc.

**Rob Mitchell**
BMW of North America, Inc.

*Motor* Magazine

**Sheri Nathanson**
Geltzer and Co., Inc.

**Ellen Parker**
Bob Thomas & Assoc.

**The Quadrant Picture Co.**

**George Rakich**
Lynch Porsche, Chicago, Ill.

**Klaus Reichert**
Porsche, Stuttgart, West Germany

**D. Randy Riggs**

**Mark A. Rollinson**
Oldsmobile Motor Division, GM Corp.

**Lee B. Sechler**
Chrysler Corp.

**Gary D. Smith**
Buick Motor Division, GM Corp.

**Vernon G. Smith**
Steve Foley Rolls-Royce, Northbrook, Ill.

**Mike Spencer**
Acura Division, American Honda Motor Co., Inc.

**George Stauffer**
Stauffer Classics, Ltd.
Blue Mounds, Wis.

**Carrie Stys**
Campbell & Co.

**Steven Tee**
L.A.T. Photographic Ltd.

**Nancy Telarico**
Hank Forssberg, Inc.

**Henry Theisens**
Lynch Porsche, Chicago, Ill.

**Steve Walzer/Mercury Marine**
Edelman Public Relations

**John Weinberger**
Continental Motors, Hinsdale, Ill.

**Susan Williams**
BMW of North America, Inc.

**Nicky Wright**

**Randy Zakem**
George Follmer Motorcars, Inc.
Montclair, Calif.

# CONTENTS

# INTRODUCTION

**Be wise with speed;**
**A fool at forty is a fool indeed**
—*Edward Young, 1725*

A walking pace—about four miles an hour—is how fast the artillery-pulling tractor built by French Army Captain Nicolas Joseph Cugnot could go. That was in 1769, and Cugnot's three-wheeled monster was the world's first steam-powered vehicle. His machine also is credited with the world's first automotive traffic accident. Cugnot rammed it into a stone wall. Indifferent to history, the authorities tossed the good captain in jail.

Thus began the great adventure. Automobiles accompanied us—and sometimes, led us—into the modern age. And like most things epochal, they were both a blessing and a burden. But their power to liberate the individual is indisputable. And their power to place true speed in the hands of the common man is a motif of the 20th Century. Today, there are moderately priced cars that easily attain 130 mph or more. A handful of the fastest production cars exceed 160 mph, and it's not uncommon that a racing machine needs to top 200 just to qualify for competition.

Of course, the term "high speed" has held a different meaning for each generation. And while the progression of higher and higher speeds has generally been steady, it is not perfectly linear.

Take Karl Benz's three-wheeler of 1885. It could hit 10 mph and generally is recognized as the first modern automobile by virtue of its 3/4 horsepower water-cooled gasoline engine. But it was not the fastest car of its day. More than a decade before Benz's creation turned its first wheel, the 10,580-pound L'Obeissante steamcar could attain a quite respectable 25 mph. It carried 12 passengers and was celebrated because it was quiet enough not to startle horses. Indeed, in these early days, the internal combustion engine was not the clearest path to high speeds. In 1899, for example, the Jenatzy, a bullet-shaped French car, set the world speed record, 65.8 mph. It was *electrically* propelled. Another French car, the Serpollet, known as the Easter Egg for its rounded shape, used a one-cylinder steam engine of 397-cubic centimeters to set a new record, 77 mph, in 1901.

Within a few years, however, the gasoline engine's compactness and reliability made it the powerplant of choice. And the speed race was on.

The 1903 Winton Bullet II had an inline 8-cylinder engine and a top speed of 84 mph. Six years later, a 21-liter 4-cylinder engine powered a Benz to a world's record 128 mph. The first car to top 200 mph was the 1927 British Sunbeam with its two 12-cylinder engines. But these were competition machines. Most road cars of the '20s had a top speed of around 50 mph; in the '30s, the average auto would do well to top 75. Sure, cars like the 1936 Bugatti 57S and the '37 Mercedes-Benz 540K would do around 120, but the Ford V-8 of 1934, with its 85-mph maximum speed, was about as hot a ride as the commoner could hope for.

Leading the top-speed charge out of World War II were the Europeans. Ferrari's 342 America of 1952 could reach 148; the Mercedes-Benz 300 SL of '54 could do more than 150. America, meanwhile, was putting horsepower into the hands of the many. Armed with its small-block V-8, a '55 Chevrolet Bel Air Sport Coupe was a 110-mph machine, while a '58 Chrysler 300 with the right gearing, a long road, and a kiss of wind behind its finned tail might touch 150.

By the early 1960s, Carroll Shelby's Ford-powered AC Cobra was rustling the leaves at 165 mph; by '67, the fastest production car in the world was probably the Lamborghini Miura, which could top 170. Ferrari's 356 GT4 Berlinetta Boxer ushered in the '70s at

more than 175 mph. America produced little that could stay with such exotics on the open road. But nobody could touch the U.S. for affordable, tire-frying acceleration! From '64 to '74, Detroit poured forth a cavalcade of big-engine coupes and sedans that could sprint from 0-60 mph in under 5.5 seconds. Pontiac Catalina 2+2, Plymouth Hemi 'Cuda, Ford Mustang Boss 429, Chevrolet 427 Corvette: mystic names from the age of the muscle car. But sky-rocketing insurance rates, and then the oil crises of the mid-1970s, pulled the plug on performance. One U.S. auto magazine in the mid-'70s ferreted out American-built cars that could double the double-nickel 55-mph national speed limit and found that in second place, behind a Corvette, was a pickup truck.

But the fuel crunch eased and automakers adapted. Cars again tripled the double-nickel, but this time with catalytic converters and gas mileage in the 20-mpg range. In the 1980s, turbochargers, multi-valve cylinder heads, and aerodynamic design helped spawn a golden new era of acceleration and top speed. THE WORLD'S FASTEST CARS celebrates this new age of speed. The thrilling machines on the pages that follow sum up what went before, and hint at much of what is to come. But even more important, they're a heck of a lot of fun!

# ACURA NS-X

**H**eart-stopping performance and a head-turning shape may get an automobile invited to the world's-fastest-car party. But balance will make that car the belle of the ball.

Supercars thrive on the notion that they don't have to do much of anything but look sharp and go fast—very, very fast. Who cares about a buckboard ride, an engine that burps and bogs at low speed, a cockpit view that hides most of the road from the driver? If you're concerned about such things, shop for a sedan.

Honda storms into the exotic-car field with its mid-engine NS-X (**below**). With a powerful, naturally aspirated V-6 and driver-friendly manner, the new car aims to add a dimension of balance often missing in the class. NS-X stands for "New sports car X," and is Honda's working title for the vehicle. The car was to get a formal name in time for its debut in Acura showrooms.

But now comes Honda, boring a hole clean through such supercar arrogance with a high-speed drill called the Acura NS-X. It's got all the performance a speed freak could dream of. It'll rip from a standing start to 60 mph in under 6 seconds. The quarter is over in less than 14. It keeps on wailing past 160 mph.

And you'll appreciate its looks as it rockets by. It runs in a classic supercar crouch, its blunted snout low to the road. Hidden headlamps introduce fenders that gracefully rise rearward, dipping midway back before swelling in the hindquarters. A discreet basket-handle spoiler tops the elegant, integrated tail. Prominent body-side vents give some hint of its mid-engine design.

But the real clue to this car's significance is its greenhouse. An unbroken parabola dominated by glass, it's perched upon the body the way a fighter plane wears its canopy. The aeronautical metaphor is no accident, for this cockpit is designed with visibility in mind. Honda, you see, believes the car should work with, not against the driver, and that includes such elemental considerations as ensuring a view good enough to take the terror out of changing lanes in midtown Manhattan. It may not sound like a big thing, but it's a philosphy by which the NS-X is helping to redefine what a supercar should be.

Indeed, NS-X stands for "New Sports car X," though Honda was to give it another name before its introduction. Its Acura surname is that of Honda's prestige division. Honda Motor President Tadashi Kume unveiled the car in February, 1989, at the Chicago Auto Show. He defined it in terms of an equilibrium foreign to most cars in the class.

"The Acura NS-X," Kume said, "was designed to provide true world-class sports-car performance and represents what we believe is the optimum balance between high-performance technology and human-fitting design." Ideally, he said, Honda would "create a sports car that will give any driver the pure pleasure of driving." That meant an agile, responsive vehicle with high levels of performance that could be enjoyed by those who didn't necessarily have advanced driving skills.

To that end, a mid-engine, rear-wheel drive layout with a transversely mounted engine was chosen for its fine blend of control and handling. With agility a goal, a heavy body was out, and so therefore was the large engine it would have required. Strictly a 2-seater, the NS-X is slightly larger than a Ferrari 328 GTB, but not quite as big as the Testarossa. Its body is an aluminum monocoque, which Honda

specified for its low weight and high strength. Curb weight is listed at 2820 pounds, quite low for the supercar class.

Mounted midships, for best balance, is a 3.0-liter V-6 with 4 valves per cylinder. Honda says it makes 270 horsepower. To afford quick throttle response and linear acceleration, Honda stayed away from turbocharging or super charging, which can inject bursts of power that sometimes cross up even experienced drivers. The transmission is a 5-speed manual.

The NS-X's all-independent suspension uses double-wishbones at all four corners. Four-wheel anti-lock disc brakes help stop it, and a traction-control system helps it to get going. Hard-core racers don't like traction control, but Honda figured this means of limiting rear-wheel spin would keep the NS-X friendly when the average driver tried to accelerate on slippery pavement. Inside, there's a driver's-side air bag.

Guiding Honda's philosophy in terms of exterior design was the placement of the greenhouse. Mid-engine cars traditionally have very limited outward visibility. But Honda's engineers placed the NS-X's canopy in the most forward position possible to provide an excellent view ahead. And unlike some mid-engine performance

NS-X styling is both beautiful and functional. A side air inlet (**opposite page**) feeds the mid-mounted 3.0-liter engine. The jet fighter-plane-inspired canopy (**top**) is designed to counter a typical shortcoming of mid-engine cars by providing a good outward view from the cockpit. In overall dimensions, the car is slightly larger than a Ferrari 328 GTB, but smaller than a Testarossa. Its mission is to deliver world-class performance to the driver of average ability.

cars, in which a glance to the rear-view mirrors reveals nothing but bodywork and air-intake scoops, the NS-X's canopy should provide the driver unobstructed visibility aft and over the shoulders. Hot, noisy cockpits and indifferent control layouts are tariffs many supercars extract in exchange for their performance. But Honda aimed for simple controls in a comfortable, airy cabin devoid of "fatigue inducing properties."

Honda has been building cars only since the mid 1960s. It jumped into Formula One racing as an infant automaker and now dominates what is arguably the world's most demanding racing class. As for passenger cars, its success with critics and buyers alike shows the company has always had a pretty clear vision of what its cars should be. It's well aware that at around $50,000-$60,000, the NS-X will be the most expensive and sophisticated Japanese production car ever. Sales projections total a modest 3,000 annually.

In the months leading up to its introduction, Honda's new sports car had the motoring world's rumor mill abuzz. Some envisioned the use of exotic materials and perhaps an adaptation of Honda's V-12 or V-10 racing engines. To be sure, the NS-X is advanced. But it is perhaps truly avant garde only in the way it treats high-performance and a friendly nature as equals. In realizing its goal of supercar power and balance, Honda may just have altered the supercar balance of power.

### Acura NS-X Major Specifications

**Manufacturer:**

Honda Motor Company, Ltd.; Tokyo, Japan

**Dimensions:**

| | |
|---|---|
| Wheelbase, in. | 98.4 |
| Overall length, in. | 169.9 |
| Overall width, in. | 70.9 |
| Overall height, in. | 46.1 |
| Track (front), in. | 59.5 |
| Track (rear), in. | 60.0 |
| Curb weight, lbs. | 2820 |

**Powertrain:**

| | |
|---|---|
| Layout: | mid-engine, rear-wheel drive |
| Engine type: | double overhead-cam V-6 |
| Displacement, liters/cubic inches | 3.0/180 |
| Horsepower @ rpm | 270 @ 7300 |
| Torque (lbs./ft.) @ rpm | 209 @ 5500 |
| Fuel delivery: | multi-point fuel injection |
| Transmission: | 5-speed manual |

**Performance:**

| | |
|---|---|
| Top speed, mph | est. 165 |
| 0-60 mph, seconds | est. 5.0 |
| Quarter-mile, seconds | est. 13.4 |

| | |
|---|---|
| **Approximate price:** | $55,000 |

*Superb handling is provided by the NS-X's mid-engine balance and light-for-the genre 2820-pound curb weight. It has an all-independent suspension, four-wheel anti-lock disc brakes, a traction control system, and manual steering. Both a 5-speed manual and an automatic transmission will be offered. A driver's-side air bag is standard. The car's appeal is its ability to go 0-60 mph in 5 seconds and top 160 mph with Honda reliability.*

# ASTON MARTIN VIRAGE

**W**hat more perfect car for James Bond? The Aston Martin DB4 with which agent 007 attacked bad guys and attracted blondes in the early '60s, was, like Her Majesty's best fictional secret servant, suave, thoroughly British, and as powerful as a gloved fist.

By the 1980s, however, the Bond character had turned to another make of sports car. Was he perhaps bored with Aston's aging offerings? It's nice to think that a ride in the new Virage would bring him back to the fold. The car has that trio of delicious Aston Martin traits: a brawny character, technological simplicity, and road-burning performance. The broad-shouldered 4000-pound coupe can run at least 155 mph and thunders from a standing start to 60 mph in six seconds flat.

England's Aston Martin unveiled its new Virage coupe at the British Birmingham Motor Show in October 1988. It wasn't a moment too soon. The proud but financially strapped automaker hadn't produced a new chassis since the late 1970s, and its Zagato models of the mid-1980s were merely limited-production indulgences for the mega-rich.

The problem, as always, was money, though to Aston's credit, it did get the Virage project underway before Ford Motor Company bought a controlling interest in the company in 1987. The first mechanical prototype of the Virage was produced early that year, disguised under a short-wheelbase version of Aston's ultra-luxury Lagonda sedan. Only four prototypes had been constructed before the public launch in October 1988.

Thoroughly British, the Virage (**left**) combines Aston Martin's classic sense of Grand Touring-car styling with a fresh design that's perfectly at home in the 1990s. The aluminum body panels are hand finished before being matched and welded to their neighbors on a master jig. Aston's thunderous 5.3-liter double overhead-cam V-8 (**above**) propels the 4000-pound coupe to 155 mph. A 0.33 drag coefficient offsets some of the weight.

The first customer cars were scheduled for delivery in June 1989, with a planned production of five cars per week. Wealthy loyalists couldn't wait, however. More than 50 deposits of at least $10,000 had been placed before the car was even unveiled.

Even with these advanced sales, Aston Martin wasn't willing to start completely from scratch for the new car. Under the new coupe body was still a front-engine chassis, still the famous 5.3 liter V-8 engine.

Though the basic layout is familiar, Project DP2034 is built on a new chassis design, and the engine itself has been given fuel injection and new 4-valve-per-cylinder heads. Not only that, but the monstrously powerful engine can now run on unleaded fuel and has a catalytic converter to help clean up the exhaust system.

Lighter and stiffer than the old V-8 frame, the box-section steel chassis is also cheaper to build. Still, a development of the old Lagonda sedan's front suspension was retained, along with an updated version of the De Dion axle seen under the Zagato.

Designed by the fashionable British partnership of John Heffernan and Ken Greenley, the new body boasts a thoroughly modern shape, yet retains traditional Aston Martin "signatures," including the familiar grille profile. Its smooth detailing contributes to a drag coefficient of 0.33. Heffernan and Greenley's design makes the car look smaller than the Aston Martin Vantage V-8, the model it is to replace. Yet the Virage is actually four inches longer and an inch wider than the Vantage, though it has no more interior space.

In fact, the cabin styling harks back to that of the 1960s-style DB4/DB5/DB6 models. The rear compartment looks inviting, with low seat cushions and rear backrests. Headroom is adequate for an adult of average size, and the generous rear quarter windows remove any sense of claustrophobia. Back-seat leg room is very tight, however. The Virage may be roomier than the V-8 or a Porsche 928, but is nonetheless no more than a 2+2.

Virage replaces Aston Martins Vantage V-8 and maintains the company's tradition of car names beginning with the letter "V." Virage means "corner" in French. More than 50 deposits of $10,000 or more were placed on it even before the $160,000-plus car was unveiled at the British Birmingham Motor Show in October 1988.

How did the car get its name? Well ahead of the launch, the company's executive chairman, Victor Gauntlett, asked many of his friends and business colleagues for suggestions. "Vulcan," "Valiant," and "Vanguard" were considered, before Gauntlett personally chose "Virage." Not only did it carry on Aston Martin's tradition for using names beginning with a "V," but it sounded continental enough ("Virage" means "corner" in French) to be chic.

As we've said, the Virage in many respects is like previous Aston Martin models. It's very powerful, it's large on the outside and rather cramped on the inside, and it is oh-so-British in concept and execution. The body is built by traditional methods. The external panels are aluminum alloy, originally pressed on simple tooling, but hand finished and individually matched and welded to their neighbors on a master jig.

High-quality wood graces the dashboard, supple Connolly leather covers the seats. The instruments are clearly marked circular dials and needles. Aston Martin, having toyed with space-age digital read-outs on the Lagonda saloon, would have no more of it for the Virage. The truly knowledgeable observer can look around the facia layout and pick out details lifted from the Ford parts bin, and Aston Martin openly admits that the car's air conditioning comes from Jaguar.

About 60 Virages per year are scheduled for shipment to the U.S., starting in December, 1989. Their price tag will read about $150,000, and no one seems to be complaining.

Virage's cabin harks back to the 1960s-era Aston Martins with straightforward instrumentation and touches of wood set amidst the aromatic leather upholstery (**left**). Big on the outside, rather cramped on the inside, the Virage's sumptuous but small rear seat (**above**) gives credence to its 2+2 label. The car is built on an all-new chassis, but retains the classic front-engine, rear-drive layout underneath its debonair and dashing exterior (**top**).

## Aston Martin Virage Major Specifications

**Manufacturer:**

Aston Martin Lagonda Ltd.; Newport Pagnell, England
(a Ford Motor Company holding)

Engine by Callaway Engineering; Old Lyme, Connecticut

**Dimensions:**

| | |
|---|---|
| Wheelbase, in. | 102.8 |
| Overall length, in. | 188.0 |
| Overall width, in. | 73.0 |
| Overall height, in. | 52.3 |
| Track (front), in. | 59.4 |
| Track (rear), in. | 59.9 |
| Curb weight, lbs. | 3947 |

**Powertrain:**

| | |
|---|---|
| Layout: | front-engine, rear-wheel drive |
| Engine type: | double overhead-cam V-8 |
| Displacement, liters/cubic inches | 5.3/326 |
| Horsepower @ rpm | 330 @ 6000 |
| Torque (lbs./ft.) @ rpm | 350 @ 4000 |
| Fuel delivery: | Weber-Marelli fuel injection |
| Transmission: | 5-speed manual or 3-speed automatic |

**Performance:**

| | |
|---|---|
| Top speed, mph | 155 |
| 0-60 mph, seconds | est. 6.0 |
| Quarter-mile, seconds | NA |

**Approximate price:** over $160,000

# ASTON MARTIN ZAGATO

Aston Martin's cars have never been mundane, but the British automaker went positively avant-garde in 1986 with the Zagato. It's a 186-mph coupe that's as brutally styled as it is brutally fast. Aston loyalists covet it in much the way Winston Churchill loved his bulldog.

Italy is famous for its automotive styling houses, each of which has its own unique character. Pininfarina's flowing forms are praised for their sensuousness. Bertone's more formal lines can be quite elegant. Zagato's cars, meanwhile, are often described as severe. To its credit, the Milan coachbuilder is seldom derivative. But its later cars are frequently festooned with bulges and creased by tormented panel cuts. Some designs border on the ungainly.

We need to point this out before describing the Aston Martin Zagato, a car with minuscule production numbers, skyrocketing value, vast performance, and polarizing looks.

In this context, we also must note that by the mid-1980s, Britain's Aston Martin was stuck in a corner. It was making so few cars, perhaps eight per week, that it was making no money. To make money it needed to sell more cars, but to sell more cars it needed new models, and to develop new models it needed to make money first.

Around 1985, Aston chairman Victor Gauntlett found a way to break this vicious cycle. Taking a page from the sales plan Ferrari used for its limited-production 1984 GTO, Gauntlett announced that Aston planned a new model, no more than 50 of which would be built. He demanded a deposit of about $27,000 with every order, even before construction began. Gauntlett said the car would retain the well-proven, long-running Aston Martin chassis and running gear, including the V-8 engine that dated from 1969. But the car would have a dramatic new Zagato body.

It was a cheeky ploy that worked. Within months Gauntlett had sold all the cars and collected roughly $1.3 million, which covered the cost of building the cars even before assembly began. The customers didn't mind. They gambled that because production was to be limited, values of Aston Martin Zagatos would rise. They turned out to be correct.

Mechanically, the Zagato's chassis is an improved version of that used under Aston's V-8 Vantage, though the engine is more powerful. This meant Zagato customers can rely on proven machinery, including a solid chassis platform, a De Dion rear suspension, and the sight, sound, and muscle of a magnificent 430-horsepower 5.3-liter four-cam eight.

Realizing that the Zagato is about 350 pounds lighter than other Aston coupes, and that the body is more aerodynamic, the company confidently quotes a top speed of 186 mph.

The design produced by Zagato could best be described as controversial. Its shape is traditional, dictated in large measure by the car's big, front-mounted engine. Beyond that, all the Zagato trademarks are present: the indelicate grille and intruding headlamps, an angular greenhouse at odds with the barrel-shaped body sides, a high beltline, a truncated tail. Invading the hood is a doorstop-shaped bulge needed to clear the four downdraft Weber carburetors. Alas, larger and more profitable companies might have installed fuel injection, or merely realigned the manifolds and fitted horizontal carburetors to eliminate the bulge, though to have done so would have cost the Zagato one of its signature features.

The first three Zagatos were rushed to completion in time for display at the Geneva Motor Show in March 1986. Zagato proceeded to patiently build the remaining 47, fitting over the Aston-built

Born of a crisis that saw Aston Martin mired in poor sales and a moribund cash flow, the Zagato is a bold declaration of the company's resolve to continue building striking automobiles. Though slightly discordant, its body is nonetheless quite dramatic (**right**). Lacking the funds to develop a lower-profile fuel-delivery system, Aston employs a four-carburetor setup that necessitates a wedge-shaped hood bulge — a welt that has become one of the Zagato's signature features. The 2-seater's luxurious interior (**left**) is well suited to high-speed driving.

With more than 400 horsepower and a top speed in excess of 175 mph, the Zagato has appeal enough. Production limited to just 50 examples cements its desirability and encourages asking prices near $500,000. An additional 25 convertible versions were built with about 100 fewer horsepower, but generated no less investor interest.

chassis its sheets of aluminum, which were hand-beaten onto wooden forms. To finish the whole batch took more than a year, by which time buyers were offering double the original purchase price of about $150,000.

Gauntlett had a winner and he wasn't about to ignore the appetite he had created among wealthy enthusiasts and investors. At the '87 Geneva Motor Show, Gauntlett announced that coupe production would indeed cease at 50, but that Zagato would now build 25 convertible versions! The droptops would have about 305 horsepower and a top speed of about 165 mph. Approximate price would be $220,000, with a $45,000 deposit. Aston's order book was filled in a matter of days.

Prices in late 1989 had climbed to $500,000, but the Zagato's appeal is not confined to its post as a limited-edition example of an historic British marque. Here is the lure of genuine supercar performance. Acceleration and top speed are well within the realm of the fastest Porsches and Ferraris of the day, plus the car has a thoroughly flexible engine. The V-8 can be trundled around town at 1000 rpm or revved happily to 6000 rpm in reliability and comfort. Its civilized manner is marred only by the high effort required to shift the beefy ZF 5-speed manual transmission.

All this, plus a hand-built body that at least does not lack for character, not to mention the luxurious air-conditioned interior of leather and wood. Strong men are reported to go weak in the knees when driving the Zagato—to own one they needed to be rich, too.

No-nonsense instrumentation (**below**) promotes a driving experience marred only by the high shift effort required by the Zagato's ZF 5-speed manual transmission. From any angle, the car displays the severe but distinctive styling that is a trademark of Italy's Zagato design house (**left**).

## Aston Martin Zagato Major Specifications

**Manufacturer:**
Aston Martin Lagonda Ltd.; Newport Pagnell, England (a Ford Motor Company holding)
Body by Zagato; Milan, Italy

**Dimensions:**

| | |
|---|---|
| Wheelbase, in. | NA |
| Overall length, in. | NA |
| Overall width, in. | NA |
| Overall height, in. | 51.0 |
| Track (front), in. | NA |
| Track (rear), in. | NA |
| Curb weight, lbs. | 3900 |

**Powertrain:**

| | |
|---|---|
| Layout: | front-engine, rear-wheel drive |
| Engine type: | double overhead-cam V-8 |
| Displacement, liters/cubic inches | 5.3/326 |
| Horsepower @ rpm | 432 @ NA |
| Torque (lbs./ft.) @ rpm | 395 @ 5100 |
| Fuel delivery: | 4 Weber carburetors |
| Transmission: | 5-speed ZF manual |

**Performance:**

| | |
|---|---|
| Top speed, mph | 185 |
| 0-60 mph, seconds | 5.2 |
| Quarter-mile, seconds | NA |

| **Approximate price:** | $150,000 ($500,000 in late 1989) |
|---|---|

# BENTLEY TURBO R

**N**ot many supercars have delicately controlled air conditioning, acres of leather seating, lots of genuine wood trim, and space to accommodate five adults *and* all their luggage for a long and luxurious holiday.

The Bentley Turbo R does.

No other of the world's fastest cars has the Bentley Turbo's combination of very high performance, enormous weight (over 5,000 pounds), subtly sporting roadholding, and dignified manner.

And this being a Bentley, it is of course extremely easy to drive fast. Simply select "D" on the transmission, bury the throttle, and the barge goes ballistic. It'll cruise at 130 mph in almost complete silence, though at such speeds it's better not to ask about fuel mileage, which can drop into single figures.

Saloon is the British term for this type of sedan. One day, perhaps, Rolls-Royce might match the Turbo's performance to a more svelte sportster. But for the moment, this tycoon's saloon will have to suffice.

For many years the Rolls-Royce automotive group held that it built the world's best cars. Its development programs were always painstaking and thorough, true, but the company never built truly fast cars. Rolls had taken over the financially troubled Bentley concern in 1931, using the newly acquired products as the basis for sportier Rolls-Royces with a different badge. These were brisk performers, but they certainly were not spine-tingling road burners. It was not until the arrival of the Bentley Mulsanne Turbo in 1982 that Rolls-Royce performance could match Rolls-Royce image and quality.

The launch of a turbo car from so auspicious a firm gave respectability to the entire cult of turbocharging that swept across Europe in the 1970s and '80s. Some people did find the very concept of a truly high-performance Bentley hard to accept. But at least there was the reassurance that Rolls-Royce had spent nearly a decade getting the technology right.

For 1987, the car was enhanced with, among other improvements, increased power, fuel injection for all markets, and sportier roadholding. The Mulsanne Turbo badge was dropped and the saloon was renamed the "Turbo R." It arrived in the United States in 1988 with a lengthy and impressive ancestry.

Bentley's Turbo R (**right**) is two-and-a-half tons of leather and fine-wood wrapped in arrogant British bodywork, a tycoon's saloon that's propelled to more than 130 mph by 6.7 liters of turbocharged and intercooled V-8 power. Discreet badging and a radiator shell painted in gloss body color, rather than a chromed unit, distinguishes the Turbo R from lesser Bentleys.

The basic chassis and complex power-assisted steering, brakes, and self-leveling suspension could be traced directly to the first-ever unibody Rolls Royce, the 1965 Silver Shadow. The light-alloy engine itself dated from 1959. It was influenced by Cadillac and Chrysler powerplants of the mid-1950s to mid-1960s. The Rolls-Royce unit copies every lazy, under-stressed habit of those pre-exhaust-emission V-8s, right down to the low rev limit and the prodigious thirst for high-octane fuel. Although a manual transmission was offered until 1965, all Roll-Royces thereafter had a General Motors GM400 automatic transmission.

In 1965, Rolls launched the Silver Shadow. With an all-independent suspension and four-wheel disc brakes, it was a truly modern design for the time. But by the end of the 1970s, it was in need of a revamp. Rolls-Royce's solution was to keep the same basic running gear, but to endow the car with a more rounded, yet still massive, four-door sedan shell. Like the old car, the modern cars had a bluff front end, with proud vertical grilles, and four headlamps. Except for a different

radiator shell, this was the Bentley of the day. Denied its individuality, Bentley sales were modest.

A change began in the early 1970s. The original turbocharged car was a prototype inspired by chief executive David Plastow in the early 1970s. But when a new generation of management set out to revamp Bentley's image, not only were the Bentley-based cars progressively given a different character, but the turbocharged car became the flagship.

The Rolls-Royce/Bentley V-8 was a rugged and simple 90-degree, overhead-valve engine displacing 412 cubic inches. In normally aspirated form with fuel injection, but in smog-controlled "California" tune, it produced about 200 horsepower with stump-pulling torque from low revs. The turbo cars used one large Garrett T04-type turbocharger. No intercooler was used because none would fit in the crowded engine bay. Original Mulsanne Turbos had a four-barrel Solex carburetor sitting in the vee of the engine, but Bosch KE injection came along in 1987. This was the fuel-injection system

already being fitted to American-market Rolls-Royces, and it made the launch of the Turbo R both logical and easy.

Except for the badging, the turbo is distinguished externally from the standard car only by its radiator shell, which is painted in gloss body color, rather than in stainless steel.

The company's discreet marketing image decrees that no peak power outputs are ever disclosed. However, West German regulations make it compulsory to admit power figures, so it's known that the carbureted version of the turbo engine produced 298 horsepower, while the fuel-injected version made 328.

The original cars could reach 140 mph, but because they were equipped with a very supple suspension they were difficult to drive fast on sinuous highways. To improve on this, Rolls-Royce introduced the R-pack (R for "Roadholding") suspension. Cynics were heard to say that the car had simply not had *any* roadholding ability before this, but they're the very ones most likely to be caught napping when the tycoon's saloon blows by.

Turbo R's cabin is stately, with burl walnut trim cut from a single tree, and leather upholstery from matched hides (**opposite page, top**). Haphazard layout of instruments and controls, however, compromises their function. Headlamp washers are standard, while the fuel-injected Rolls-Royce engine (**opposite page, bottom**) generates 328 horsepower. Handling and roadholding are outstanding for a large car. The body's relatively narrow width and a commanding seating position help the driver maneuver the Bentley.

## Bentley Turbo R Major Specifications

**Manufacturer:**

Rolls-Royce Motors Ltd; Crewe, England

**Dimensions:**

| | |
|---|---|
| Wheelbase, in. | 120.5 |
| Overall length, in. | 207.4 |
| Overall width, in. | 79.0 |
| Overall height, in. | 58.7 |
| Track (front), in. | 61.0 |
| Track (rear), in. | 61.0 |
| Curb weight, lbs. | 5270 |

**Powertrain:**

| | |
|---|---|
| Layout: | front-engine, rear-wheel drive |
| Engine type: | turbocharged, intercooled V-8 |
| Displacement, liters/cubic inches | 6.7/412 |
| Horsepower @ rpm | est. 328 @ 3800 |
| Torque (lbs./ft.) @ rpm | est. 487 @ 2400 |
| Fuel delivery: | port fuel injection |
| Transmission: | 3-speed automatic |

**Performance:**

| | |
|---|---|
| Top speed, mph | over 135 |
| 0-60 mph, seconds | 6.7 |
| Quarter-mile, seconds | 15.7 |

| **Approximate price:** | $149,500 |
|---|---|

Despite its regal bearing and stratospheric price, the Bentley Turbo R lacks some world-class attributes found in most other top-line European sedans. Its firm ride lacks suppleness and a few rattles disturb the cabin's tranquility. Still, it's got an inescapable classicism, and there's nothing else like it for ruffling the feathers of cars that look sportier, but can't deliver the goods when the throttle goes down.

# BMW 750iL

omination is the byword for BMW's magnificent flagship. The 750iL dominates poor pavement, other traffic, and the gods of gravity and momentum. It has the capacity to isolate occupants from every outside unpleasantness while furnishing the driver with excellent feedback from the road. It's also confident and understated. The exterior is smoothly sculpted, almost austere. At more than $70,000 the 750iL is no bargain, but it is clearly a benchmark. A magnificent 5.0-liter V-12 beneath the hood makes it so.

BMW's flagship 7-Series first reached the U.S. in early 1987 as the 111.5-inch-wheelbase 735i with a 208-horsepower inline 6-cylinder engine. A year later, the top-of-the-line 750iL (**below**) bowed. It boasts a V-12, modified grille, and a 116-inch wheelbase, with the extra length going into the rear-seat area. It stickers at $70,000 and carries an $1850 gas guzzler tax.

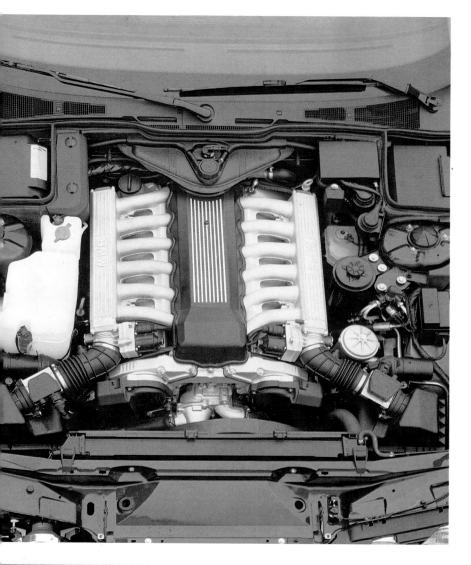

Companies like Auburn, Cadillac, and Hispano Suiza had built such engines in the 1930s, and Ferrari made them famous in the 1940s, but it took Jaguar in the early 1970s to prove that "V-12" and "volume production" could be mentioned in the same sentence. BMW had designed several V-12 engines during the '70s, but never put them into production. It was only word that arch-rival Mercedes-Benz was planning such an engine that inspired BMW to unveil its 12 in 1987.

The vehicle chosen to accept the engine was the new 7-Series sedan. The car had been launched in the U.S. in the spring of 1987 as the 735i, with a 3.5-liter inline six. It's the first of a generation of BMWs with the rounded styling that will take the marque into the 1990s.

The 7-Series for the '90s is a large and heavy car. It is in every way an answer to what Mercedes-Benz thought it did best with the S-Class, and it aims to be more refined, more comfortable, and more capable than any other car in the world. Standard equipment includes an all-independent suspension, four-wheel anti-lock disc brakes, and a plethora of electronic engine controls and power convenience features. Some months after the 735i came the 750iL, meaning 7-Series, 5.0-liter engine, and fuel injection in a wheelbase 4.5 inches longer than the 735i's. Compared with the six-cylinder 7-Series cars, the 750iL has a slightly different shape to its front grille, twin squared-off tailpipes, and forged (instead of cast) alloy wheels. It also has upgraded brakes, a self-leveling rear suspension, and increased-capacity engine and oil cooling systems. The only transmission offered on the 750iL is a ZF 4HP24 4-speed overdrive automatic.

The 750iL's 24-valve, single-overhead camshaft all-aluminum engine arranges its cylinders in a 60-degree vee. Lift the hood and you're confronted with a dozen light-alloy inlet pipes and a central air-intake spine proudly displaying the BMW badge. There seems little space for accessories, all of which are tucked away under the sides of the cylinder block.

The 750iL weighs a hefty 4235 pounds—190 more than a contemporary Cadillac Brougham—but it has one horsepower for every 14.1 pounds of curb weight, a better power-to-weight ratio than the M3 or M5 and only an eyelash behind BMW's best, the M6 (13.9). The V-12 makes 48 percent more horsepower than the 735i's 3.5-liter six.

Styling of the 750iL (**opposite page**) is typically BMW, but more rounded and aerodynamic than the previous 7-Series. Heart of the 750iL is the 24-valve, single overhead-cam, aluminum-block V-12 (**this page**). Its 300 horsepower is enough to hurtle the 4235-pound Bimmer from 0–60 mph in 7.2 seconds and to an electronically limited 155 mph.

Top speed is 155 mph, limited by the electronic controls of the Motronic engine management system. The car surges effortlessly to 100 mph in less than 20 seconds, which puts it well into the supercar category. There is torque enough to snap your head back, but also the ability to summon what feels like an endless rush of horsepower. The engine is very flexible, allowing the big Bimmer to leap ahead in effortless strides, reeling in highway traffic or jumping through gaps in rush-hour commuters.

At idle the engine is almost silent and without vibration, ticking away like a sewing machine. At 70 mph, the car is whisper quiet, with wind a subdued hiss around the front roof pillars and freeway expansion joints a gentle "pock" beneath the tires. The suspension feels impervious to road imperfections—stable and supremely absorbent, never floaty or weak-kneed. Drivers find themselves seeking out the ugliest pavement just to marvel at how the 750iL refuses to allow its body or occupants to be disturbed. There is some body roll in corners, but great grip from Pirelli P600 225/60VR15 tires. Torque is sufficient enough to pull the sedan through long, fast sweeping turns in a neutral stance or to induce a dose of oversteer in sharper corners. An invaluable aid to handling in a car this large is the ability to place the vehicle. Here, the 750iL's high seating position and relatively short hood and narrow body work in concert with its fine manners to let the driver maneuver with aplomb at any speed.

Simple, businesslike, and precise describes the cockpit and the controls. The car is exceedingly comfortable, with an air of superior assembly and design contributing to its composed cabin atmosphere. The front seats have modest-looking side bolsters, but afford surprising support in fast turns. The rear compartment is limousine-like, the trunk huge. Storage bins are sprinkled about the cabin.

Romantics might scoff that, as with similar Mercedes-Benz cars, the 750iL is so capable, so fast, so effortless, and so efficient that it has developed its own Teutonic character of soulless competence. Perhaps they could never learn to love a 750iL. For others, an ultra-safe car capable of long, fast journeys in complete comfort, one that rewards in a score of subtle and overt ways, is its own romance.

The 750iL (**top and right**) is BMW's answer to the Mercedes-Benz S-Class sedan. BMW set out to make it more refined, more comfortable, and more capable than its German competitor, and perhaps it has—the 750iL has been rated the world's best sedan by much of the world's motoring press. A dismantled engine (**above**) shows the complexity of BMW's V-12. Word has it that a 4-valve-per-cylinder version is due sometime in the future.

## BMW 750iL Major Specifications

**Manufacturer:**

Bayerische Motoren Werke AG; Munich, West Germany

**Dimensions:**

| | |
|---|---|
| Wheelbase, in. | 116.0 |
| Overall length, in. | 197.8 |
| Overall width, in. | 72.6 |
| Overall height, in. | 55.1 |
| Track (front), in. | 60.2 |
| Track (rear), in. | 61.3 |
| Curb weight, lbs. | 4235 |

**Powertrain:**

| | |
|---|---|
| Layout: | front-engine, rear-wheel drive |
| Engine type: | single overhead-cam V-12 |
| Displacement, liters/cubic inches | 5.0/304 |
| Horsepower @ rpm | 296 @ 5200 |
| Torque (lbs./ft.) @ rpm | 332 @ 4100 |
| Fuel delivery: | LH-Jetronic fuel injection |
| Transmission: | 4-speed automatic |

**Performance:**

| | |
|---|---|
| Top speed, mph | 155 |
| 0-60 mph, seconds | 7.2 |
| Quarter-mile, seconds | 15.2 |

**Approximate price:** $70,000

# BMW M3

One horsepower per cubic inch. It's a magic-sounding ratio that begs the attention even of those with a passing interest in performance cars. What about, say, 192 horsepower from, oh, 140 cubic inches of naturally aspirated engine? That's pure sorcery, enough to demand the attention even of the hardcore enthusiast. It's also enough to pass most performance cars. That's BMW's spirited M3.

Here's a sedan that doesn't appear much different from a standard 3-series 2-door. But look more closely. Its body has a slight rake, its fenders bulge around fatter 205/55V15 tires running on 7-inch-wide rims. A small spoiler tops the tail. Turn the key. The engine doesn't hum, it burbles. Slip it into gear. Already the suspension feels tauter than that of a standard 3-Series car, the steering a tad sharper. Upshift. Run it to 3500 rpm. The engine's music is changing, from throaty to a rasp. The car leaps ahead at the slightest movement of your toe on the accelerator. Upshift. The engine is wailing now, egging you on toward the 7250-rpm redline. Throw the car into a turn, conquer the curve, slingshot into the straightaway, top 100 mph in less than 20 seconds. You're running 140 now, unperturbed and arrow straight. Press the brake pedal. Feel the shoulder belt bite as you're hauled to a stop with undiluted authority. Do it again.

Some cars have motorsport built into them. Some come to excel in the sport. Others will never make it, however hard they try. For two decades BMW has been making nicely engineered road cars which, with a great deal of effort, could be turned into race- or rally-winning cars. It was not until 1986, however, that the West German company produced the M3, its first "homologation special."

In Europe, there's an important series of races and high-speed rallies intended for nearly stock production cars. Highly publicized and closely contested, it's called "Group A." To qualify for Group A

BMW's M3 (**above**) was built for competition in European "Group A" racing, which mandates only slightly modified production cars. BMW qualified the M3 for the class by building at least 5000 units, then kept it on as a regular production model. It boasts leather sports seats, full instrumentation, even air conditioning (**opposite page**).

recognition, a car must have four full-sized seats and at least 5,000 examples must be made in one year. Most European automakers are represented in the series by cars modified into racers. But a few—notably Ford of Europe, Lancia, and BMW—build special cars for Group A. Hence the M3.

BMW is nothing if not thorough. Almost as soon as the revised 3-Series range had been launched in the early 1980s, the engineers began working on the M3 project, but four years were needed to make it ready for sale. Not only were the first 5,000 cars built and sold quickly, but the M3 was retained as a regular production machine. "Homologated" for motorsport use at the beginning 1987, the M3 immediately proved to be competitive, though it was usually defeated

The M3 looks much like a regular 3-Series BMW, but the body has a slight rake and employs fender bulges, a decklid spoiler, and other aero aids. The 2.3-liter four (**left**) features Bosch fuel injection, twin overhead cams, and 4 valves per cylinder. It cranks out 192 horses—an impressive 1.37 horsepower per cubic inch.

by the much more powerful Ford Sierra RS Cosworth.

The secret of M3's performance is under the hood, where, surprisingly enough, there is a 2.3-liter 4-cylinder engine instead of the inline 2.5-liter six used in other U.S. 3-Series BMWs. BMW, it turns out, had looked at the Group A regulations, worked out the weights and likely roadholding "balance" of various cars, and decided that the four was right.

But what a four. Based on BMW's Formula 1 racing engine, its alloy cylinder head has twin overhead-camshafts, four valves per cylinder, and Bosch fuel injection. The result, in road-car tune, is a rip-snorting 192 horsepower pulling 2750 pounds.

It would, of course, have been possible to produce a turbocharged unit (the BMW 2002 Turbo of 1973, after all, was Europe's original turbocharged road car), but that would have moved the car into another motorsport class, so the idea was discarded.

For all its wonderful power and elan, the M3 does have some compromises in street use. The 5-speed gearbox is by Getrag, and is by no means as quiet and refined as BMW would like. But BMW used

it because, for motorsport purposes, it could be fitted with other ratios. The race-bred high-compression engine in conjunction with a 4.10:1 final-drive ratio makes for raucous turnpike cruising, even if the sound is consistent with the car's character. If the power-assisted rack-and-pinion steering seems a touch slow, it might be because at the three-digit speeds for which the M3 was designed, faster steering makes for twitchy control. You can take the M3 off the Autobahn, but you can't take the Autobahn out of the M3.

Although definitely one of the world's fastest cars, the M3 has to be hustled along to make its point. The engine is happier when being revved hard than when being cosseted, and the handling, though well-balanced and extremely safe, somehow feels more poised when being powered through a corner. In twisty conditions the M3 is one of the most agile of all such "homologation specials."

The interior is furnished for such serious business, with leather-upholstered sports seats, standard air conditioning, a premium stereo system, and a full array of unobstructed gauges. Clearly, the M3 offers the best of more than one world.

## BMW M3 Major Specifications

**Manufacturer:**
Bayerische Motoren Werke AG; Munich, West Germany

**Dimensions:**

| | |
|---|---|
| Wheelbase, in. | 101.0 |
| Overall length, in. | 171.1 |
| Overall width, in. | 66.1 |
| Overall height, in. | 53.9 |
| Track (front), in. | 55.6 |
| Track (rear), in. | 56.1 |
| Curb weight, lbs. | 2865 |

**Powertrain:**

| | |
|---|---|
| Layout: | front-engine, rear-wheel drive |
| Engine type: | double overhead-cam inline 4-cylinder |
| Displacement, liters/cubic inches | 2.3/140 |
| Horsepower @ rpm | 192 @ 6750 |
| Torque (lbs./ft.) @ rpm | 170 @ 4750 |
| Fuel delivery: | Bosch Motronic fuel injection |
| Transmission: | 5-speed manual |

**Performance:**

| | |
|---|---|
| Top speed, mph | 143 |
| 0-60 mph, seconds | 7.6 |
| Quarter-mile, seconds | 15.4 |
| **Approximate price:** | $34,950 |

Although the M3 provides a comfortable cabin (**top center**), it almost demands to be hustled along. Its engine thrives on high revs and the handling feels more poised when the car is being powered through a corner. A Sunday driver will never appreciate the M3, but an enthusiast who knows how to wring the maximum performance out of a car will find it a delightful challenge.

# BMW M5

**F**ast cars tend to come in one of two forms: striking or subdued. BMW's latest M5, like its predecessor, clearly falls into the latter class. A car that looks so much like a sedate family carrier couldn't possibly hold blazing road potential under its hood, could it?

Yes, it could. And does. Externally, there's little to show that *this* 5-Series car, first sold only in Europe, will run 15 mph faster than any of its mates in the BMW stable. Only the exquisitely detailed 17-inch-diameter magnesium alloy road wheels and the oh-so-discreet "M5" badges at front and rear give the game away.

If the former M5 (produced until 1988) was fast, this slightly bigger descendant is an all-out sizzler. Start with a 0-60 mph time of 6.3 seconds. Throw in a top end around 155 mph—and that's because a speed-limiter kicks in (said to be a safety feature for the tires). The result: a performance machine that has few rivals on any nation's roads.

*Automobile* magazine has called the M5 "the fastest factory-tuned sedan money can buy," adding that it "combines magnetic roadholding and inspired handling with a level of ride comfort even Grandma could live with." *Car and Driver* is even more succinct in its praise, referring to the European M5 as "the baddest Bimmer of the bunch," a car that "leaps to the top of the BMW performance class."

Just where in the world does adding the letter "M" to the front of a perfectly normal car name turn a smart sporting sedan into a supremely rapid road burner? Where else but Munich, the West German capital of Bavaria, where BMW builds its renowned series of exquisite motorcars.

Car and Driver says the BMW M5 (**both pages**) is "the baddest Bimmer of the bunch." True, for here's a family sedan that charges from 0-60 mph in a mere 6.3 seconds and offers superbly balanced handling, to boot. BMW's on-board engine-management computer caps the M5's top speed at 155 mph as agreed upon by West German automakers to placate those who would restrict speeds on Germany's speed-limitless Autobahn.

The modern family of BMWs stems from the company's rebirth in the early 1960s, when the boxy 1500 went on sale. There was nothing remarkable about that car's looks or its chassis, but the all-new overhead camshaft 4-cylinder engine was right up to date.

Since then, BMW has developed 6-cylinder versions of that engine, including a new smaller "six" that uses many elements of the first one. That original straight-six was launched in 1968. Now a highly developed version of that design powers BMW's stunningly attractive M5.

The letter "M" stands for "Motorsport." Then again, some might contend that it also stands for "Muscle." BMW's Motorsport division not only produces cars and engines specifically to win races and rallies, but also as the ultimate in fast road transport. West Germany, unlike most other countries, still has no maximum speed limit on the main *Autobahns*, and the M5 was developed to take full advantage of that.

The original 5-Series BMWs were launched in 1972, then dramatically facelifted in 1981. Not until 1987 did an all-new, second generation 5-Series appear. Like its bigger cousin, the latest 7-Series, it was a smooth, carefully profiled car developed with fanatical care and attention to detail.

In the early 1980s, there had been an M5 derivative of the existing 5-Series models. BMW's motorsport department, which totaled 400 engineers by 1988, wanted the new-generation M5 to be a company flagship—more sporting and quite a lot smaller than the 750iL, which was also making headlines at the time. So in that same year, BMW was ready to show its modern interpretation of the same 4-door sedan theme. Under the hood went a 216-cubic-inch (3.5-liter) six churning out no less than 315 horsepower. That's 55 horsepower more than offered in the previous-generation M5. Most surprising, that output is produced with or without a catalytic converter in the exhaust system.

The latest M5 has a top speed claimed to be at least 155 mph. Even that mark is limited by the electronic cutout, so the true top might well approach 170 mph!

Top speed is no small matter in West Germany, because the M5's rating puts it within an ace of the most powerful Porsches and ahead of the whole Mercedes-Benz bunch. BMW also has shown itself more than a match for the handful of Jaguars and other imported exotica that stray into that fiercely nationalistic nation.

The secret behind the M5's colossal performance is its engine, of course, a further-tuned version of the twin-overhead camshaft, 4-valve-per-cylinder jewel, previously sold only in the memorable, limited-production M1 coupe. For the M635CSi model (also described

Based on the 5-Series sedans introduced in 1988, the design of the current M5 (**foreground**) is an evolutionary development of its predecessor (**center in photo**), which was based on the 1981-'87 5-Series cars. The new M5 gets 315 horsepower from the same dohc, 3.5-liter six that made 256 horsepower in the old M5. The engine is derived from the 277-horsepower unit in the legendary, limited-production mid-engine M1 (**background**).

in this book), the engine has been slightly enlarged, with a longer stroke. Further development has produced an output of 1.45 horespower per cubic inch—a stunning level for a normally aspirated engine. Even better, the latest version is, like all such BMWs, silky smooth, flexible, and devoid of temperament.

Behind the flywheel stands a big and beefy 5-speed all-synchromesh gear box supplied by Getrag, the same basic type used in Jaguars and large BMWs. The basic car is BMW's modern 5-Series body shell, still with four passenger doors, a beautifully equipped interior, and generous 5-seater accommodation. Styling touches include a lowered nose and the raised, cut-off tail that was introduced with the new-generation 7-Series cars. Up front is a small slotted air dam; at the sides, modest rocker extensions.

Down at chassis level, the M5 uses a MacPherson strut front suspension, semi-trailing independent rear suspension, and massive front and rear disc brakes (anti-lock standard). All this results in the sort of ride and handling balance that only Mercedes-Benz and Jaguar seem able to match, and an almost uncanny poise in all conditions.

Although still a heavy car by BMW standards (if not by Detroit standards) at 3,700 pounds, an M5 can be tossed around as nimbly as its smaller cousin, the race-intended M3. BMW tested both cars separately around the incredibly twisty and long "old" Nurburgring race circuits. The M5 lost little or nothing in the corners, and was topped by the more nimble M3 only in the sprint and brake tests.

Compared with the "ordinary" 5-Series cars, the M5 has a lowered and stiffened suspension, larger and wider-rim wheels with fat (234/45 section) tires, but a totally low-key and understated character—until roused by the driver.

Once the driver starts to reach for higher performance, the M5's potential rises up in readiness. The 24-valve engine tickles and burbles its way through traffic until unleashed, then howls lustily up to an electronically controlled rev limit of 7200 rpm. Because the final drive incorporates a limited-slip mechanism, traction is always good, even out of corners. An M5 hurls its way from one obstruction or tight corner to the next.

As confirmed by those who tested the first cars, the M5 is almost *unreasonably* good, and feels as if it could carry on delivering such enormous performance in all weather, in all climates, in all countries. Except for its agility, however, many pundits feel it will be completely wasted in the U.S. That remains to be seen as a limited number of the reworked M5 arrive on U.S. shores.

## BMW M5 Major Specifications

**Manufacturer:**

Bayerische Motoren Werke AG; Munich, West Germany

**Dimensions:**

| | |
|---|---|
| Wheelbase, in. | 108.7 |
| Overall length, in. | 185.8 |
| Overall width, in. | 68.9 |
| Overall height, in. | 54.8 |
| Track (front), in. | 58.0 |
| Track (rear), in. | 58.9 |
| Curb weight, lbs. | 3680 |

**Powertrain:**

| | |
|---|---|
| Layout: | front-engine, rear-wheel drive |
| Engine type: | double overhead-cam inline 6-cylinder |
| Displacement, liters/cubic inches | 3.5/216 |
| Horsepower @ rpm | 315 @ 6900 |
| Torque (lbs./ft.) @ rpm | 260 @ 4750 |
| Fuel delivery: | Bosch Motronic fuel injection |
| Transmission: | 5-speed manual |

**Performance:**

| | |
|---|---|
| Top speed, mph | 156 |
| 0-60 mph, seconds | est. 6.3 |
| Quarter-mile, seconds | NA |

**Approximate price:** est. $54,500

One of the world's great engines: the 24-valve BMW inline six (**opposite page**). Its 1.45-horsepower per cubic inch is a stunning output for a naturally aspirated engine. Laid out for the serious driver, the BMW's instruments and controls (**above**) meet the high standards set by the M5.

# BMW M6

**S**uperlative speeds and stark appointments need not go hand in hand. BMW's biggest M-Series super coupe is proof of that, combining performance and luxury in one mighty pretty package. Relating his road-test experiences in *Car and Driver*, Csaba Csere noted that "the big coupe sets no performance standards, but it's as satisfying to drive as any of the legendary speedsters." No records may have been set, but a top-end that passes 140 mph with ease, coupled with acceleration to 60 mph in well under 7 seconds,

The BMW M6 is a latter-day variation of the 6-Series coupe that dates to 1976. It's intended for the enthusiast who wants a car about halfway between a racer and a grand tourer. The M6 fits the bill perfectly. The handsome coupe does 0-60 mph in 6.8 seconds and tops out at 156 mph. It has a firm, no-compromise suspension. Yet it has all the luxury features anyone could desire.

doesn't exactly put the M6 in the automotive bush leagues, either.

To BMW, the prospect of this kind of car was irresistible. On the one hand, the company was building a smart and beautifully engineered, if rather conventional, 2+2 coupe. On the other, it had a magnificent race-proved twin-cam engine of the right size and shape. Fitting the pair together seemed an obvious goal. The result is the 150-mph M6.

The story begins in 1976, with the launch of the new 6-Series. There was only one coupe body style, offering "almost 4-seater" accommodations, independent suspension at front and rear, 4-wheel disc brakes, and a greater stock of electronic gear. There were two engine sizes, each with a single overhead-valve layout, six cylinders in line, and Bosch fuel injection. By the late 1970s the engine had grown to 209-cubic inches (3.43-liters), pushing out more than 200 horsepower, to give the solidly-built Bimmer coupe a top speed past 130 mph. It was fast, it was safe, it was beautifully built. But it wasn't a supercar.

Meanwhile, BMW took a detour toward the limited-production mid-engined M1 coupe. Although this one had chassis, suspension, and body assemblies designed in Italy, the engine was pure BMW—a twin-cam conversion of the original "straight-six," with 4-valves per cylinder. But—and this was typically BMW—it was not a straight conversion. The variant engine used a stouter crankshaft and rods, stronger pistons, deeper block, subtly different bore/stroke ratio, and revised manifolding. The proof, of course, came in its 286-horsepower output—far above the usual 220 horsepower or so; and with more torque, too, developed higher up the rev range.

The 6-Series coupes were big and bluff-fronted, with traditional rather than "aerodynamic" styling. Still, they were easily recognizable machines. A long, low hood covered that impressive straight-six engine, with the famous kidney-style front grille motif, topped by the

similarly famous BMW badge. A large trunk was specially designed for this class of car, and no one could complain about the level of equipment. But it *still* wasn't a supercar—not yet, at least.

Help was on the way. Even though BMW was committed to building Grand Prix engines in the early 1980s, it remained interested in touring-car racing. This interest turned into the excuse for matching the M1's fine engine to the 6-Series car's equally superb structure. The result, announced in mid-1983, was the M635CSi—and if it isn't obvious, we should point out that in BMW language "M" stands for "Motorsport." That's the BMW division responsible for the big performer—and a few little performers as well.

The new car is a strange mixture—not really enough M-for-Motorsport, but not quite enough "Touring Car," either. It's powerful, for sure. Squeezing 286 horsepower out of a non-turbocharged 211-cubic-inch/3.45-liter "six" is outstanding by any normally aspirated standards. The newest "M" is also a heavy car, 3,500 pounds, loaded with equipment. Except for different alloy wheels and obviously larger tires, the only real evidence of "M-Power" up front is revealed by the "M" badges on the front grille and on the tail.

Several oddities make the car difficult to categorize. For one, the engine is as smooth as silk at low revs, but by no means silent. It ticks and rumbles as it gathers speed, then positively howls as it approaches peak revs (nearly 7000 rpm). In standard form, there's more to this powerplant, as its pull-from-anywhere character affirms. It seems to say, "I have no temperament—thrash me and see how I can ignore the punishment."

Other 6-Series cars were sold with stick shift or automatic transmission, but not the M635CSi. "M-Power" customers could get only a 5-speed Getrag gearbox, with a lower back-axle ring gear setting to allow for the much higher-revving twin-cam engine.

Like all such supercars, the M635CSi makes a mockery of open-road speed limits, in America and elsewhere. Naturally, that makes it ideally suited to blasting up and down West Germany's limit-free *Autobahns*. The car's top speed of 150 mph might not be seen often. But on fast highways it is easy (and very pleasurable) to rush up to 130 mph and beyond, drop back to a mere 80 mph or so to clear an obstruction, then shift down to fourth, or even to third (whose maximum was a straight 100 mph) to disappear rapidly toward the horizon.

For all that speed potential, the car is beautifully finished and sumptuously equipped, with acres of high-quality leather, deep pile carpets, a fully trimmed trunk, and some glossy decorator touches. On the other hand, it rides hard, bumping and clattering over potholes and lane indicators.

Handling, however, is always impeccable. The fat 240/45-section tires (mounted on BBS-style wheels) rarely seem to let go, and the power-assisted ball-and-nut steering is ideally weighted for its job.

The M635CSi, in other words, is the sort of BMW a wealthy enthusiast might buy if he didn't want to put up with the foibles of a Ferrari. It's a good choice, too, if said enthusiast doesn't want to keep other cars in his garage for use while the expensive toy is being serviced or repaired.

BMW's planners decided that the ride should be as harsh as it is, that the exhaust note is there for a reason; so owners accept such quirks. Fans love the linking of 150-mph performance to all the established BMW virtues—beautifully fitting panelwork, meticulously detailed service and maintenance schedules, computer control of the engine's fuel injection systems, and electronically sensed anti-lock brakes as standard. Best of all is the car's ever-present character as a properly and accurately developed vehicle, designed to go on pleasing its owners year after year.

When the big Bimmer coupe hit American shores three years after introduction in Europe, it dropped the last portion of its moniker, becoming plain "M6." Horsepower dropped down as well, to 256 at 6500 rpm, in order to meet U.S. standards. That restricted top speed to 144 mph or so, as opposed to the 150-mph capability of its close European cousin. Acceleration doesn't seem to suffer, though, according to figures reported by U.S. road testers. In either guise, this is high-speed motoring in the luxury mode.

*The M6's ride may be harsh, but the handling is always impeccable, helped in part by the fat 240/45-section tires mounted on BBS-style wheels and the precise, ideally weighted ball-and-nut steering. Anti-lock brakes are standard.*

## BMW M6 Major Specifications

**Manufacturer:**

Bayerische Motoren Werke AG; Munich, West Germany

**Dimensions:**

| | |
|---|---|
| Wheelbase, in. | 103.3 |
| Overall length, in. | 189.6 |
| Overall width, in. | 67.9 |
| Overall height, in. | 53.3 |
| Track (front), in. | 56.3 |
| Track (rear), in. | 57.7 |
| Curb weight, lbs. | 3570 |

**Powertrain:**

| | |
|---|---|
| Layout: | front-engine, rear-wheel drive |
| Engine type: | double overhead-cam inline 6-cylinder |
| Displacement, liters/cubic inches | 3.5/211 |
| Horsepower @ rpm | 256 @ 6500 |
| Torque (lbs./ft.) @ rpm | 242 @ 4500 |
| Fuel delivery: | Bosch Motronic fuel injection |
| Transmission: | 5-speed manual |

**Performance:**

| | |
|---|---|
| Top speed, mph | 156 |
| 0-60 mph, seconds | 6.8 |
| Quarter-mile, seconds | 16.1 |

| | |
|---|---|
| **Approximate price:** | $55,950 (1988) |

The replacement for the long lived 6-Series, both the M6 and the 635CSi, is the 850i. Like the 6-Series, the 850i serves as BMW's flagship coupe. Initially, it comes only with the 7-Series 300-horsepower V-12, although 6-cylinder versions may show up later. Much of the chassis is derived from the 7-Series sedans and the length is only a few inches greater than the M6. List price is expected to top $70,000.

# BUICK
# GNX

**A**lthough known for sedate family sedans, Buick has issued its share of sizzlers over the years. Quickest and starkest of the lot is the GNX, the last of a storied breed: the rear-drive GM muscle car. Introduced for only the 1987 model year, the GNX was a hotter version of Buick's already hot Grand National. Only 500 GNXs were built, all of them painted black, all of them now legends. Think 0-60 mph in well under 6 seconds. Think 100 mph in the quarter-mile from a mid-sized American coupe. You're thinking GNX.

Long after big-block V-8 engines faded into history, the Grand National and its GNX descendant were a throwback to the days of rear-drive muscle cars. Back in the 1960s, Buick offered the "Gentlemen's Express," the fabulously styled and fast Wildcat. Then came the Gran Sport Skylark, flaunting the muscle-car theme of big engines and smaller bodies. Grand finale of that era was the 455-cubic-inch GSX (Gran Sport-X), a car whose production ended before some performance enthusiasts knew it even existed. The GSX was one of the most spectacular of all the muscle cars and as quick as any production automobile of its time.

Building on that glory was the Grand National, introduced in 1985. Here's what the original GN did for *Car and Driver* evaluators: "Grand National will scream from 0-to-60 mph faster than any other car made in America. Is 4.9 seconds fast enough? ... The GN even outsprints two of Ferrari's blue bloods—the Testarossa (5.0 seconds) and the GTO (5.1 seconds) —both of which we tested in European specification."

As if that weren't enough, Buick let loose with both barrels in 1987 with the GNX. In its short life, the GNX was, simply, the fastest production car offered in this country.

As it happened, the GNX also was the supreme finale of the rear-wheel-drive Regals. Buick dropped them for a new line of front-wheel-drive Regals in 1988.

Planning for the "X" concept began in April of 1986 when David Sharpe, Buick's chief engineer, asked the man in charge of advanced concepts, Mike Doble, to develop a special version of the Grand National to salute the end of an era. Doble and Project engineer Chuck Jensen were in charge of producing the prototype GNX. That car became a collaborative program, spearheaded by Buick, with two other Michigan firms: Automobile Specialty Company of Southgate and McLaren Engines in Livonia.

ASC's past efforts for Buick had included such limited-edition vehicles as the 1982-85 Riviera convertible. McLaren had a long history of winning race cars and had done engine work on the Buick-powered 1985 Indy 500 pole-sitter and Buick's modern-day concept car, the Wildcat.

*The Detroit muscle car went out in a blaze of tire-smoking glory with the Buick GNX (left). Retaining the classic muscle-car theme of a powerful engine in an otherwise mundane mid-size coupe, the baddest Buick of all is one of the fastest accelerating cars ever, capable of quarter-mile runs in the mid-13-second range. Produced in a limited edition of 500, the GNX is the ultimate expression of the only slightly tamer Buick Grand National.*

a thoroughbred machine for the enthusiast. The GNX fender vents harken to the Buick trademark portholes. The GNX's, however, are functional, boosting airflow through both the intercooler and radiator.

Under the hood remains Buick's sequential-port fuel-injected V-6, similar to that offered in a number of the division's cars. To take that extra step toward all-out performance, though, the GNX sports an improved ceramic turbine-wheel turbocharger, a more efficient intercooler, and a reprogrammed computer memory chip for better full-throttle characteristics. The car also has cylinder heads with increased flow efficiency and an auxiliary transmission oil cooler.

Suspension tweaks include 16-inch aluminum alloy wheels to replace the GN's 15-inchers, along with Goodyear 130-mph-plus-rated Eagle VR "Gatorback" radial tires, a modified rear suspension, and flared wheel-well lips. Inside, the car features full analog instrumentation and a handsome sports layout of articulated seats and a console-mounted automatic-transmission shifter.

The last Grand National rolled down GM's "G-Car" assembly line in Pontiac, Michigan on December 11, 1987. Buick's target was to build the quickest GM production sedan ever made. Bull's eye!

*All GNXs are painted black and ride on stylish 16-inch alloy wheels (**opposite page, top**). The stock Buick buckets are treated to a special contrasting color scheme with the Grand National turbo logo sewn onto the headrests (**opposite page, bottom**). Muscle cars traditionally used big V-8 engines, but the GNX's turbo V-6 (**bottom**) makes up for its relative lack of cubic inches with mountains of high-tech, computer-enhanced horsepower.*

## Buick GNX Major Specifications

**Manufacturer:**

Buick Motor Divison and ASC Inc.; Southgate, Michigan

McLaren Engines; Livonia, Michigan

**Dimensions:**

| | |
|---|---|
| Wheelbase, in. | 108.1 |
| Overall length, in. | 200.6 |
| Overall width, in. | 75.5 |
| Overall height, in. | 54.6 |
| Track (front), in. | 59.4 |
| Track (rear), in. | 59.3 |
| Curb weight, lbs. | 3545 |

**Powertrain:**

| | |
|---|---|
| Layout: | front-engine, rear-wheel drive |
| Engine type: | turbocharged, intercooled overhead-valve V-6 |
| Displacement, liters/cubic inches | 3.8/231 |
| Horsepower @ rpm | 300 @ 4400 |
| Torque (lbs./ft.) @ rpm | 380 @ 2600 |
| Fuel delivery: | sequential port fuel injection |
| Transmission: | 4-speed automatic |

**Performance:**

| | |
|---|---|
| Top speed, mph | 124 |
| 0-60 mph, seconds | 4.7 |
| Quarter-mile, seconds | 13.4 |

**Approximate price:** $27,000

# CALLAWAY SLEDGEHAMMER CORVETTE

**S**ome people are never satisfied. When it comes to super-powered automobiles—especially Corvettes—Reeves Callaway is one fellow who seldom is. "What would it take," wondered this wizard of the turbo-tuned sports car, "to build a 250 mph automobile?" The answer: a Sledgehammer.

Coming from the creator of the formidable Callaway Twin Turbo Corvette, the idea of an "ultimate" street 'Vette is more than a mental exercise. Callaway's first Twin Turbo Corvette, developed in 1986, already was a legend for taking the stock Chevy's top speed from an impressive 150 mph and stretching it to around 180, with sub-5-second 0-60-mph times and 13-second quarter-miles thrown in for good measure.

Well-heeled hotfoots heard the call, and rushed to their Chevy dealers, where the Callaway Twin Turbo was available as a regular production option. All 185 Callaway Twin Turbos built in 1987 found buyers within six weeks of car's announcement. Production expanded in 1988, as did the urge for something even wilder. When a German aftermarket tuner, AMG, created a 186-mph hot-rod Mercedes-Benz and dubbed it the "Hammer," the gauntlet was tossed. Callaway, in American one-ups-manship, decided his 250-mph Corvette would merit nothing less than the moniker, "Sledgehammer."

The Sledgehammer saga began in June, 1988, in Callaway's headquarters in Old Lyme, Connecticut. Reeves Callaway has developed aftermarket turbo applications for BMW, Volkswagen,

and Alfa-Romeo cars since the late 1970s. But his highest-profile handiwork has always been on Corvettes. The Twin Turbo car had garnered its share of notoriety. But Callaway realized that the next step—toward 250 mph—was a big one. For his full-nuclear 'Vette, Callaway put together a team composed of chief engineer Tim Good, project engineer Elmer Coy, and project technician Dave Hendricks. Engineering assistance was provided by Talbot Hack.

Tony Cicale, from Carl Haas' Indycar team, was the consulting aerodynamicist. Extensive chassis development was turned over to Carroll Smith, whose three decades of experience proved invaluable. But generally, the platform of the production Corvette was retained. The team was confident that it was strong enough to handle the highly stressed conditions of 250-mph speed tests. One final question was whom to put behind the wheel. Callaway was the man, though drag racer John Lingenfelter of Ft. Wayne was tapped for additional driving chores.

*A fully streetable Corvette capable of going 250 mph was the not-so-modest goal of aftermarket modifier Reeves Callaway. His solution is the Sledgehammer (**both pages**), a twin-turbo 'Vette whose name—and top speed—go the 186-mph Mercedes-Benz 6.0 Hammer one better.*

Once the project got underway, its extreme technical requirements became apparent. Taking a fully streetable car from normal traffic conditions to more than 250 mph reached well beyond any prior achievements. How much horsepower would be needed? What sort of spark plug would work? How would heat rejection be achieved? What aerodynamic assistance was necessary? Which tires could handle the job?

In addition, time had to be scheduled at the vast 7.5-mile highbanked Transportation Research Center (TRC) track in Ohio. Once that commitment was made, everything had to be right.

Callaway's firm consists of just 30 people, a rather small army for such a major battle. As word of their 250-mph intentions got around, though, existing American hardware and know-how from outside corporations was made available. Now, the Sledgehammer was more than just a high-speed test for Callaway. It had become a high-speed testbed for the nation's finest technology.

A significant breakthrough was provided by the Champion Spark Plug Company with their H.O.T. (High Output Technology) sparkplugs. Champion produced a new-generation igniter that can idle indefinitely, then go to 250 mph without fouling—even when boost pressure goes from ambient to 22 psi. Such combustion requirements all the way from low-end to high-end mean enormous variance in physical conditions. Sledgehammer offered Champion its first opportunity to test its most modern development, which fuses aircraft, marine, and automotive technology in plugs that may soon reach the public.

Very extensive modifications, including boost pressure of around 15 psi and a radical cam, brought a Callaway-modified 350-cubic-inch, 4-bolt-main Corvette engine up to 1,013 horsepower.

To improve driveability, however, that plan was abandoned in favor of a mild cam and the higher boost pressure. The flexibility of Callaway's turbocharger technology was invaluable. It allowed a "detuned" engine of 898 horsepower that turned the ultra-potent Sledgehammer into a surprisingly docile cruiser when the car was driven 700 miles from the Callaway plant to the TRC track. The return trip through a sleet storm was uneventful.

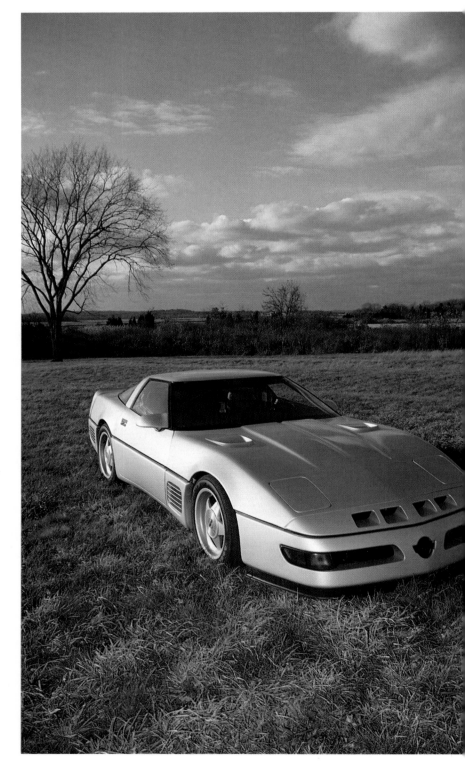

The Sledgehammer uses two Turbinetics TO4B turbochargers, each mounted just aft of the front wheels, behind the 'Vette's gill-like body openings. The largest possible turbo intercoolers are located up front with ducted airflow from four vents. Brodix heads with Jesel roller rockers, held by Jesel stud girdles, provide valve control. Crower rods with Callaway-designed Cosworth pistons deliver power to a custom crankshaft and driveline. The entire Sledgehammer driveline is made up of special Dana components—similar to Callaway pieces but of stronger material, shotpeened and magnafluxed along with stronger connector pieces. Rochester fuel-injected combustion is controlled by a Zytec engine management system, firing through an MSD (Multiple Spark Discharge) ignition. That's the heart of Sledgehammer.

Handling the heat load of such a powerful engine is the chore of Mobil 1 synthetic oil, the only oil that Callaway recommends for his cars. Lubricant heat rejection comes from heat exchangers located in the front fender-well areas on both sides of the car. Lubricant for the full-race-prepared Doug Nash 5-speed manual transmission (with overdrive unit) and the rear axles are cooled by heat exchangers located behind rear-wheel grill openings.

All that, and the Sledgehammer is air conditioned, too! Its condenser is behind the driver's-side rear-wheel grille opening. Other amenities mirror those of the regular Callaway Corvette, including leather upholstery, power windows, plush carpeting, and a cassette player. The Sledgehammer adds a roll cage, fire system, and 5-point safety harness.

One spin-off of the project was increased aerodynamic efficiency, in the form of the Callaway Aerobody. Callaway plans to offer the Aerobody package to the public. Paul Deutschman designed the aerodynamic front, rear, and side panels, which give any 1984 and

The Callaway-modified 350-cube Corvette engine (**opposite page, bottom**) is boosted by two turbos to 880 horsepower. Nose vents and carefully tuned bodywork (**this page**) aid cooling and roadholding, while Callaway-developed side vents (**opposite page, top right**) relieve the engine bay of air pressure and heat. Chevy-sanctioned Callaway cars are part of the regular Corvette option sheet.

newer Corvette an altogether different look. But the panels, priced at about $5,000 complete, offer more than flashy styling. Fabricated from Xenoy XT, the most advanced GE thermoformed plastic available for automotive use, they have strength, yet are deformable while holding paint far better than fiberglass.

So how did all this planning and new technology turn out? You decide. Lingenfelter strapped himself into the Corvette, fired the engine, waited for the oil to heat and for the Goodyear ZR40 Gatorbacks to warm, and then he nailed it. *One-hundred and sixty miles per hour.* The turbos wailed and the engine roared. *One-ninety.* Wind, cheated by the aero bodywork, rushed furiously past the cockpit windows. *Two-twenty.* Down, now, down TRC's long, long straightaway. *Two forty.* Lingenfelter howled into range of the timing devices, foot to the floorboard, fingers wrapped tightly around the thick, leather steering-wheel rim. The Corvette rocketed through the speed traps. The red liquid crystal display in the black box at trackside read 254.76 mph. Behold the world's fastest Corvette. As if that weren't enough, no car had ever gone faster at TRC.

The beauty in all of this is that the Sledgehammer is a streetable car that's maintained close ties to its pure-stock roots. The same can't be said of the others in this league, the Porsche 959 and Ferrari F40. They're European ultra-exotics conceived as race cars and put on the street only to satisfy homologation rules. And the Sledgehammer is still some 50 mph faster than either. Nice job, Reeves.

*Callaway offers an aerobody package of plastic exterior panels (**opposite page**) to dress up and streamline any 1984 or newer 'Vette. Behold the world's fasted Corvette (**above**). The Sledgehammer turned 254.76 mph on the vast 7.5-mile highbanked Transportation Research Center track in Ohio. Several U.S. automotive-equipment companies teamed with Callaway to develop the Sledgehammer.*

## Callaway Sledgehammer Twin Turbo Corvette Major Specifications

**Manufacturer:**
Callaway Cars; Old Lyme, Connecticut

**Dimensions:**

| | |
|---|---:|
| Wheelbase, in. | 96.2 |
| Overall length, in. | 176.5 |
| Overall width, in. | 71.0 |
| Overall height, in. | 46.7 |
| Track (front), in. | 59.6 |
| Track (rear), in. | 60.4 |
| Curb weight, lbs. | est. 3350 |

**Powertrain:**

| | |
|---|---:|
| Layout: | front-engine, rear-wheel drive |
| Engine type: | twin turbocharged overhead-valve V-8 |
| Displacement, liters/cubic inches | 5.7/350 |
| Horsepower @ rpm | 880 @ 6250 |
| Torque (lbs./ft.) @ rpm | 772 @ 5250 |
| Fuel delivery: | electronic fuel injection |
| Transmission: | 5- or 6-speed manual |

**Performance:**

| | |
|---|---:|
| Top speed, mph | 254.76 |
| 0-60 mph, seconds | 3.5 |
| Quarter-mile, seconds | 10.3 |

| **Approximate price:** | $350,000 |
|---|---:|

# CORVETTE GTP

oday's most advanced Corvette isn't fit for the road. It is instead bred for the ultra-demanding Camel GT pro circuit. Its turbocharged V-6 may be smaller than the familiar old V-8, but this is no car for the faint of heart. Even the most avid street Corvette fans would struggle to cope with their favorite's race-track alter-ego.

Imagine hurtling past the pits at Le Mans, taking the fast right-hander, then the esses and onto the Mulsanne Straight. Take it up

The Corvette GTP was bred to enhance Chevy's image—and to race in settings such as the 24 Hours of Le Mans (European Group C) and in the IMSA GTPrototype series. It carries the Lola chassis designation T-710 and runs with a turbo V-6 good for 700-900 horsepower. To maintain product identification, the T-710 follows the styling lines of the production Corvette.

through the gears to flat out, perhaps kissing 250 mph. Then brake hard and downshift to 45 for the kink at the end. Roar out of the turn followed by two dozen of the fastest cars in existence, in the hands of the most capable drivers in the world. Then left and right through the turns named Indianapolis and Arnage, fast as you can. Lap after lap around the 8.36-mile French circuit, for 24 hours, day and night, rain or shine, for some 7,000 gear shifts.

This is the world of the Corvette Grand Touring Prototype. It's purpose is twofold: to enhance Chevrolet's performance reputation by racing the 24 Hours of Le Mans and other Group C events on the European calendar and America's own International Motor Sport Association (IMSA) GTPrototype series; and to further develop Chevrolet's 90-degree V-6 engine technology.

It has triumphed on both counts, but in the fast-forward universe of racing development, Chevrolet has learned that long-term GTP success is illusive.

This unique Corvette traces its lineage to the V-8 Chevrolet-powered Lola T-600 of 1981. The Cooke-Woods team Lola T-600 was the first ground-effects coupe ever built and incorporated so much new technology that it dominated the GTP series in its debut season. Brian Redman drove the very first one built to the '81 IMSA GTP championship.

Today's Corvette GTP carries Lola chassis designation T-710 and was fabricated in the shops of Eric Broadley's famed Lola Cars, Ltd. in Huntington, England. The turbo V-6 T-710 is smaller and lighter than the V-8-powered T-600, yet it produces more power. Top speed is similar, but the turbocharged Corvette GTP accelerates quicker. Also, the V-6 car's lower overall weight offers the dual benefits of reduced stress, thus lighter parts, and faster speeds through turns. End result: reduced lap times.

In order to maintain product identification, the T-710 follows the styling lines of the production Corvette, though the GTP has a 106.5-inch wheelbase compared to the street car's 96.2. The GTP body is also about a foot longer, primarily because of its extended nose, an aerodynamic snout that clears the ground by just 2.5 inches.

The car's chassis centers around a monocoque main section that uses aircraft-technology aluminum panels sandwiching lightweight honeycomb aluminum. One interesting feature of the suspension's advanced push-rod and rocker-arm design is that a lever in the cockpit allows the driver to alter the angular position of the rocker blades, thus controlling the car's anti-roll capacity. With 16-inch diameter tires, 23.5 inches wide in the front and 27.0 at the rear, the GTP Corvette can exceed .2g lateral acceleration—more than twice the capability of a production Corvette.

The cars also differ in the field of aerodynamics. Because street cars are considerably heavier and usually driven at modest speeds, they need to be superior wind cheaters. Therefore, the production Corvette's drag coefficient of 0.341 indicates a very slick design. By contrast, the GTP Corvette has the dual need of minimum air resistance in the straightaways and maximum downforce in the turns. The GTP's design takes these dual requirements into account. Its flat underbody incorporates a venturi rising from the underbody and exiting between the rear wheelwell extensions to create a low-pressure area. Acting as an inverted aerofoil, the GTP shape and large wing keep the car glued to the ground.

The GTP body is made of high-strength Kevlar fabric bonded with epoxy resin. NACA-type ducts admit cooling air and vent high-pressure areas. The left side inlet feeds air to the turbocharger intercooler and to the engine oil cooler. The right side inlet feeds the single large engine radiator and transaxle oil cooler.

The heavy-duty cast iron V-6 block is an adaptation of the 90-degree engine used in a variety of production GM cars, although displacement is reduced to 209 cubic inches from the standard 231. Stroke is reduced from 3.48 inches to 2.75, while bore is increased to 4.0 inches (from 3.74) to produce a more favorable over-square form. The block, cast aluminum heads and internal components are all over-the-counter parts, listed in Chevrolet's heavy-duty parts catalog. The heads are closed-chamber design with 64-cubic centimeter volume, delivering a modest compression ratio of 7.5:1.

A compact Warner-Ishi Model RX9-L turbocharger provides maximum boost of 20 psi. Horsepower was 775 as first raced. Output was later increased to around 900 horsepower. With a Hewland VG 5-speed transaxle, the 1,950-pound GTP Corvette proved a formidable machine.

It snared the pole at the Daytona 24 Hours of 1986. The turbo-missile won the pole position at Road Atlanta later that year, setting a new track record of 124.998 mph while qualifying. It went on to finish first in the 313-mile event, establishing a new race average of 120.951 mph. This win broke a string of 16 Porsche victories and put an American make in the winner's circle for the first time in years.

*The Corvette GTP body is made of high-strength Kevlar fabric bonded with epoxy resin. NACA-type ducts admit cooling air and vent high-pressure areas. The left-side inlet feeds the turbo intercooler and engine oil cooler; the right, the engine radiator and transaxle oil cooler.*

Then came the Grand Prix of Palm Beach and another Corvette GTP victory. Both Road Atlanta and Palm Beach were in the string of seven Corvette GTP pole position performances, a new IMSA record. The following year, 1987, looked to be a good one for the Hendrick Motorsport GTP Corvettes. They were quick, as usual, setting four poles and three race fastest laps. But they rarely went the distance, with no wins, and they finished a distant second place to Porsche in the manufacturer's point standings. For 1988, the cars got updated V-8 power and improved by about three seconds per lap—but so did competitors. The year was dismal, with no wins and a fourth-place finish in IMSA manufacturer's points. No one can take away the victories already recorded by the Corvette GTP. But with consistent success growing rare, those trophies serve as a symbol for its engineers, crews, and drivers that winning is always within reach.

The Corvette GTP (**opposite, top**) broke a run of 16 Porsche victories when it took the checkered flag at Road Atlanta in 1986. The block of the heavy-duty V-6 (**opposite, bottom**) is an adaptation of the 90-degree engine used in GM production cars. The cockpit (**below**) reflects the strictly business nature of the Corvette GTP.

## Chevrolet Corvette GTP Major Specifications

**Manufacturer:**

Lola Cars Ltd.; Huntington, England

**Dimensions:**

| | |
|---|---|
| Wheelbase, in. | 106.5 |
| Overall length, in. | 188.0 |
| Overall width, in. | 79.0 |
| Overall height, in. | 41.0 |
| Track (front), in. | 63.0 |
| Track (rear), in. | 61.0 |
| Curb weight, lbs. | 2009 |

**Powertrain:**

| | |
|---|---|
| Layout: | mid-engine, rear-wheel drive |
| Engine type: | turbocharged V-6 |
| Displacement, liters/cubic inches | 3.4/209 or 3.0/183 |
| Horsepower | 700-900 |
| Torque (lbs./ft.) | 510-570 |
| Fuel delivery: | multi-point fuel injection |
| Transmission: | 5-speed manual |

**Performance:**

| | |
|---|---|
| Top speed, mph | 220-plus |
| 0-60 mph, seconds | NA |
| Quarter-mile, seconds | NA |

| | |
|---|---|
| **Approximate price:** | $200,000 (1987) |

# CHEVROLET CORVETTE ZR-1

The Corvette ZR-1 came to be called the "King of the Hill" by Chevy insiders while it was being developed. While that title isn't officially used by Chevrolet, it expresses the nature of the ZR-1 so well that everyone else has adopted it.

The doctrine of Corvette as the affordable American car capable of putting fancy foreign sports jobs to shame is a religion at Chevrolet. From this creed springs the Corvette ZR-1, muscling its way into the domain of Porsches, Ferraris, and Lamborghinis, heralded by Chevy as nothing less than the world's fastest production car.

That claim is debatable, but the ZR-1 is most assuredly the world's fastest production Corvette. It reaches 60 mph from a standing start in 4.5 seconds, rips through the quarter-mile in 12.8, and keeps on running all the way to 180 mph. Awed Chevy insiders took to calling their new bullet the "King of the Hill."

Though only practiced eyes will be able to discern the modest exterior changes that distinguish the ZR-1 from a run-of-the-mill Corvette coupe, there's plenty under the skin that's out of the ordinary. An all-aluminum 350-cubic-inch Lotus-designed V-8 breathes through 32 valves and generates 380 horsepower at 6200 rpm and 370 pounds/feet of torque at 4200. A six-speed manual gearbox is mandatory. An adjustable suspension keeps the ZR-1's steamroller tires on the road and helps it achieve a racer-like 1g reading on the skid pad.

Chevy's script for this ground-breaking new Corvette casts it in several roles. In one, it's a docile everyday two-seater; in another, it's a road-burning dervish. A subplot has it playing the cheerleader, stirring up excitement that GM hopes will rub off on the rest of the Chevrolet line. Indeed, the Corvette has been lighting Chevy wicks since the car's 1953 debut. The most exciting 'Vettes have always been the highest-performance versions, and these are the very cars that make up the ZR-1's family tree. Technically, the ZR-1 is not a distinct Corvette model but a Regular Production Option (RPO). It's the latest in a long line of extra-cost packages and individual components designated by a Chevrolet code system that assigns an "L" to engines, an "M" to transmissions, and a "Z" to suspensions.

A king has no need to flaunt fancy attire, and so it is with the "King of the Hill," which looks much like the regular 'Vette. Indeed, in one of its roles, it **is** a docile everyday 2-seater; in its other, it's a road-burning dervish.

Celebrated RPOs include the 1963 Z06, a Sting Ray with a 306-horsepower, fuel-injected 327-cubic-inch V-8, race-bred brakes and suspension pieces, and an available 36-gallon fuel tank. The ultimate for '67 was the famous L88, a 427-cubic-inch/560-horsepower monster whose 12.5:1 compression ratio demanded 103-octane fuel. The LT1 arrived for '70 as a solid-lifter version of the 350 Chevy small block. Rated conservatively at 370 horsepower, it formed the basis for a competition package that was the original ZR1.

Today's ZR-1 traces its genesis to the early 1980s, when Chevy began soliciting outside firms for an engine that would be a "quantum leap" in small-block performance. In the spring of 1985, as GM was preparing to buy England's Group Lotus, Tony Rudd met with the Corvette Group to discuss putting Lotus 4-valve heads on the 'Vette's 5.7-liter V-8. Rudd, managing director of the British sports-car maker, eventually counterproposed a fresh approach: an all-new engine that would meet Chevrolet's performance, emissions, and economy targets. Thus was born the powerplant Chevy labels the LT5, heir to a long and storied line of L-badged performance engines.

The LT5 is assembled in Oklahoma City by Mercury Marine under a contract with GM. Designed to fit in the standard Corvette engine compartment, the LT5 makes 50 percent more horsepower than the base push-rod 5.7-liter L98 engine. It has sequential fuel injection, an 11.0:1 compression ratio, 4 valves per cylinder, and dual overhead cams (four in all), each pair driven by a steel roller chain. A computer selectively dispenses flow to primary and secondary intake ports to give tractability under 3500 rpm and good breathing at higher rpm. A rev limiter kicks in at around 7000 rpm.

One of the ZR-1's unique features is its so-called "valet key." Located on the center console, the valet key is a kind of security blanket for the owner who might occasionally entrust the car to someone else. In its "Normal" position, the key runs the engine on its primary intake ports only. This limits horsepower to just below the L98's 245. Its "Full Engine Power" position allows secondary-valve operation, unleashing maximum 32-valve muscle.

Despite the ZR-1's performance, it meets the federal city/highway standard of 22.5 mpg and thereby escapes a gas-guzzler tax. Fuel efficiency is enhanced by a unique feature of the new ZF 6-speed manual gear box: In light-throttle applications, a computer activates a pin in the linkage that blocks shifts from first to second gear. Instead, the pin bumps the shift lever from first directly into fourth gear. With heavier throttle pressure, the computer allows normal shifting through all the gears. Fifth and sixth gears are overdrive and the LT5 turns only 1600 rpm at 65 mph.

**Opposite page**: The ZR-1 is more than content to provide fun-in-the-sun pleasure (**opposite page, top**), but it's equally ready to leap to 60 mph in a mere 4.5 seconds (**opposite page, bottom**). Note the square taillights and the bulged rear fenders, the ZR-1's main exterior distinctions. **This page**: The cutaway shows how the King's drivetrain is arranged.

Standard is the Z51 Performance Handling Package, which includes heavy-duty springs and stabilizer bars, upgraded 4-wheel anti-lock disc brakes, and a power-steering cooler. Also tacked on to the standard 'Vette's 4-wheel independent suspension is the new FX3 Delco-Bilstein Selective Ride Control, by which the driver can adjust shock-absorber damping between Touring, Sport, or Competition modes. ZR-1s will also get Chevy's new low-tire-pressure warning system that continuously monitors the air pressure in each tire while the vehicle is being driven.

ZR-1s have Corvette's standard-size 275/40ZR-17 Goodyear Eagle tires in front, but use massive 315/35ZR-17 unidirectional Eagles at the back. The ZR-1's rear fiberglass had to be modified to clear the wider rear rubber. Starting from the door and extending rearward, the ZR-1's fenders bow slightly, adding three inches of width and one inch of length to the standard 'Vette's aft proportions. ZR-1s also have a convex instead of concave rear body panel and rectangular taillamps instead of round ones. Curb weight is 3466 pounds, 236 more than a standard '89 Corvette coupe.

In the best tradition of exotic motor cars, the ZR-1 is a veritable racer-for-the-street. Its moves are competition-car sharp, its bearing billiard-table stable. Its engine and brakes are so strong that a passenger finds his noggin glued to the headrest under full throttle, his torso tipped forward in hard stops. And the sound of a wide-open LT5 is automotive opera. Even at a list price of $59,000, the ZR-1 is true to the Corvette ethic: Acquiring these thrills anywhere else would cost thousands more dollars. Americans have little use for royalty, but this is one "king" that is red, white, and blue.

**Opposite page:** The ZR-1 was introduced to the press in southern France (**top left**). The King has a big heart: a Lotus-designed 5.7-liter, double-overhead-cam, 4-valves-per-cylinder aluminum V-8. It's good for 380 horsepower. **This page:** The view from this cockpit costs $58,995.

## Chevrolet Corvette ZR-1 Major Specifications

**Manufacturer:**

Chevrolet Motor Divison; Warren, Michigan

Engine built by Mercury Marine, Stillwater, Oklahoma, from a design by Group Lotus of Great Britain

**Dimensions:**

| | |
|---|---|
| Wheelbase, in. | 96.2 |
| Overall length, in. | 177.4 |
| Overall width, in. | 74.0 |
| Overall height, in. | 46.7 |
| Track (front), in. | 59.6 |
| Track (rear), in. | 61.9 |
| Curb weight, lbs. | 3440 |

**Powertrain:**

| | |
|---|---|
| Layout: | front-engine, rear-wheel drive |
| Engine type: | double overhead-cam V-8 |
| Displacement, liters/cubic inches | 5.7/350 |
| Horsepower @ rpm | 380 @ 6200 |
| Torque (lbs./ft.) @ rpm | 370 @ 4200 |
| Fuel delivery: | twin-port fuel injection |
| Transmission: | 6-speed manual |

**Performance:**

| | |
|---|---|
| Top speed, mph | 180 |
| 0-60 mph, seconds | 4.5 |
| Quarter-mile, seconds | 12.8 |
| **Approximate price:** | $58,995 |

# CHEVROLET/PENSKE PC-18

The PC-18 Indycar is a study in balance and force. The wedge-shaped rocket took Rick Mears (**below**) to his unprecedented fifth pole position at Indianapolis in 1989 with the fastest qualifying speeds ever for the "500:" a one-lap mark of 224.254 mph, and a four-lap record of 223.885. Emerson Fittipaldi, who qualified third behind Al Unser, Sr.'s PC-18, won the race in another PC-18.

**A** sea of humanity rises as one to cheer the most spine-tingling sight in motorsports: a snarling pack of open-wheel racers converging on the green flag at the Indianapolis 500. Leading the wave as it swoops out of turn four and screams down the front straight are the three cars with the fastest qualifying times. At Indianapolis, that means *averaging* more than 223 mph for four laps of the hallowed 2.5-mile oval. No cars have so dominated this sought-after trio of slots as the charges from the garages of Roger Penske. From 1977 through 1989, Penske-team cars sat on the Indy pole eight times. Penske-built PC-17s, in fact, snared all three front-row positions in 1988 and his PC-18s did it again in '89.

The PC-18, the new dominant force in Indycar racing, rides a chassis designed by Britisher Nigel Bennett and built by Indycar czar Roger Penske. Its heart, however, is the Ilmore Chevrolet Indy V-8, a reliable 720-horsepower warhead that's coveted by rival teams.

Starting at the front is one thing, of course. Finishing there is quite another. But here again, no one has been so successful as Roger Penske. With seven victories between 1972 and 1988, his drivers have won more Indianapolis 500s than anybody's. Penske-built cars have been winners as well, starting with the Penske chassis that carried Rick Mears to his first Indy victory in 1979. Bobby Unser won with a PC-9B in '81, Mears got his third Indy victory with a PC-17 in '88, and Emerson Fittipaldi grabbed the '89 checkered flag in today's state-of-the-Indy-art PC-18.

In some ways, the PC-18's success story really began in April 1986, when a Penske PC-15 driven by Al Unser debuted an engine that has changed the face of Indycar racing: the Ilmore Chevrolet Indy V-8.

Until 1979, Penske's Indy machines used primarily McLaren or March chassis powered by Offenhauser or Cosworth engines. He retained Cosworth power even after going primarily to his own chassis. In late 1983, however, Penske encouraged two former Cosworth engineers, Mario Illien and Paul Morgan, to lay plans for an all-new engine. Penske persuaded Chevrolet Motor Division to back

the newly formed Ilmore Engineering with massive and essential infusions of money and technical support. The contract signed in 1984 by Penske, Chevy, Illien, and Morgan specified that the jointly developed new engine would be called the Chevrolet Indy V-8.

The engine has become the hot ticket in Indycar racing. Its first win was in April 1987, powering Mario Andretti at Long Beach. The Ilmore Chevy swept the first seven races on the Indycar calendar in '88, a year in which six of the first nine Brickyard qualifiers used the engine, including winner Rick Mears. Emerson Fittipaldi's '89 Indy 500 win was with the Chevy, the second straight year that Indy's entire front row was Ilmore powered.

Displacing the rules-mandated 2.65 liters (161 cubic inches) and burning 1.8 gallons of 100 percent methanol per mile, the double overhead-cam, turbocharged Ilmore Chevy can pump out 720 horsepower at a wailing 11,000 rpm. Still, it's not always the most powerful engine in an Indycar field. The stock-block Buick, for instance, is thought to be capable of more horsepower. But Ilmore's secret is lightness, compactness, and reliability. Its one-piece, sand cast, heat treated aluminum block weighs only 325 pounds, including the clutch. That's about 40 pounds less than a Cosworth. A very stiff, tunnel-type sump casting doubles as a structural member of the chassis. Light magnesium alloy camshaft covers double as upper engine mounts. The connecting rods are fully machined alloy steel forgings and there's titanium in the valve train for extremely light weight. The connecting-rod bolts are smaller than those of conventional engines without sacrificing strength. A substantially oversquare design of 88.0-millimeter bore and 54.4-mm stroke minimizes stress and promotes endurance. Finally, an innovative fuel and air induction system locates the plenum inlet deep in the engine's vee, resulting in a lower profile for better aerodynamics.

Chevy has been very selective in choosing which teams are allowed to buy the Ilmore engine. And although the V-8 has been fitted to both March and Lola chassis, it's been most effective in the Penske chassis. Penske, in fact, developed his PC-15 concurrent with the Ilmore engine. It's important to note that neither the Ilmore nor

the PC-15 was a smashing success from the start. It wasn't until the Ilmore Chevy was mated to the Penske PC-17 in 1988 that the combination became a consistent winner. The successful PC-17 of '88 was designed by Nigel Bennett, who had formerly shaped Lola's Indy cars. Before the '89 season began, Bennett supervised rigorous testing of his newest creation, a refinement of the PC-17 so dramatic, that the British-born designer regards the PC-18 as a separate and distinct race car.

"The PC-18 is a totally new car with virtually no common parts with the PC-17," Bennett says. "The PC-18 has improved aerodynamics, stiffness, more favorable distribution of mass, etc."

Penske Racing in Reading, Pennsylvania, prepares the cars, which were driven in '89 by some of the biggest names in Indycar racing: Mears, Fittipaldi, Danny Sullivan, and Al Unser, Sr. The PC-18 is a study in balance and force, a wedge-shaped rocket that took Mears to an unprecedented fifth pole position at Indy with the fastest qualifying speeds ever for the "500:" a one-lap mark of 224.254 mph, and a four-lap record of 223.885.

The PC-18 starts with a monocoque chassis of aluminum and carbon fiber that houses a 40-gallon Goodyear Crashworthy fuel cell and supports an all-independent, push-rod suspension. Its body is shaped by Penske using data gathered after testing a 40-percent scale model in the rolling-road wind tunnel at England's Southampton University and after running full-scale cars at General Motors' wind tunnel in Michigan. A variety of wings, air foils, even wheel designs, is used. Forty-one percent of the PC-18's weight rests on its front wheels, 59 percent on its rears. The steering is rack and pinion, a quick one turn lock-to-lock. Because of the need to back up, PC-18s running on road courses use a 5-speed manual transmission; oval trackers employ a gearbox with six forward speeds and no reverse.

Fifteen-inch diameter wheels are used front and rear, but the front tires are 25 inches in diameter and 9.5 inches wide, while the rears are 27 inches in diameter and 14 inches wide. The PC-18 makes use of a computer to monitor 28 separate functions. One of the most important is fuel mileage. A fuel gauge in the car tells how much fuel remains,

but the computer plots the on-board fuel supply against the race mpg and against how much fuel remains in the pit-side tank. From this, it calculates the first lap on which the car can enter the pits without costing an extra fuel stop late in the race. A second number shows the last lap the car can pit without running out of fuel on the track. Mears used the system in the Phoenix 200. He defied convention by skipping a fuel stop during a yellow caution. He later pitted under green to lose a lap. Then he unlapped himself and won the race by passing Al Unser, Jr., whose car ran dry within sight of the checkered flag.

Racers often talk of unlocking the speed in their cars. It's as though they believe that if they could somehow communicate with the car in its language, they could make it go faster. Microprocessors like the PC-18's are a step in this direction. But the people with the fastest cars seem to have reached a certain uncanny understanding on their own. Here's Mears on Bennett, the PC-18's designer: "One night at dinner, I brought up something that happened on the track that day, and Nigel began dissecting the entire car, explaining what was happening to each component in the suspension, relating that to the balance of the car, telling everything in great detail yet concisely, like he was a computer reading out the life story of the car. When he was finished, he had painted a beautiful picture, with every piece laid out, yet with everything in its place."

*Knowing when to pit and then getting the work done quickly is vital to Indycar success (**opposite page**). PC-18 pit-stop intervals are determined with the help of a computer that calculates fuel consumption. Indycars compete on twisty road courses (**above**), and on high-speed ovals. PC-18s running on road courses use a 5-speed manual transmission; oval trackers employ a gearbox with six forward speeds and no reverse gear.*

## Chevrolet/Penske PC-18 Major Specifications

**Manufacturer:**

Penske Cars Ltd., Poole, Dorset, England
Engine built by Ilmore Engineering Ltd., Brixworth, England

**Dimensions:**

| | |
|---|---|
| Wheelbase, in. | 112.0/115.0 |
| Overall length, in. | 184.0 |
| Overall width, in. | 78.5 |
| Overall height, in. | 36.0 |
| Track (front), in. | 68.0 |
| Track (rear), in. | 64.0 |
| Curb weight, lbs. | 1550 |

**Powertrain:**

| | |
|---|---|
| Layout: | rear-engine, rear-wheel drive |
| Engine type: | turbocharged double overhead-cam V-8 |
| Displacement, liters/cubic inches | 2.6/161 |
| Horsepower @ rpm | 720 @ 10,750 |
| Torque (lbs./ft.) @ rpm | 365 @ 8500 |
| Fuel delivery: | Ilmore electronic/mechanical fuel injection |
| Transmission: | (oval tracks) 6-speed manual (road courses) 5-speed manual |

**Performance:**

| | |
|---|---|
| Top speed, mph | 240 |
| 0-60 mph, seconds | NA |
| Quarter-mile, seconds | NA |

| | |
|---|---|
| **Approximate price:** | NA |

# CHEVROLET NASCAR LUMINA

A NASCAR Winston Cup stock car can cover the length of a football field in *one* second; a mile takes only 17 seconds. Racing at 210 mph demands razor-honed driving skills, absolute concentration, and nerves of steel.

In stock-car racing's major league, running up front also requires quality machinery and lots of teamwork. Darrell Waltrip has the talent, the car, and the crew it takes to win. By 1989, the Tennessean had snared three Winston Cup championship titles, all in a Chevrolet Monte Carlo SS—the winningest model in the history of NASCAR. Waltrip started the '89 season in a Monte Carlo and won the Daytona 500. He was first across the finish line at Atlanta and Martinsville, also. But the trusty SS was retired before the big race at Talledega. Its replacement was Chevy's new Lumina coupe.

In its debut at Talledega International Raceway, Waltrip's '90 Lumina hinted that it might indeed be worthy of someday wearing the Monte

Chevrolet's 1990 Lumina coupe (**below**) is one of NASCAR's newest and fastest cars, capable of 190-plus runs. Carburetor plates mandated on the fastest tracks reduce horsepower, however, so the nervy business of drafting and slingshotting (**opposite page, top**) is elevated to an art form. With aerodynamics vital to winning, wind-tunnel tests are used to fine tune the Lumina with spoilers and strategically placed air foils (**opposite page, bottom**). They balance downforce against straight-line, high-speed penetration.

Carlo's crown. Waltrip qualified his new mount in fifth spot on the starting grid with a speed of 189.959 mph, and came home fifth in the race.

If the Lumina proved its worth on that maiden voyage, it didn't take long to prove it could win. At the very next—and longest—race on the NASCAR schedule, the Coca-Cola 600 at Charlotte Motor Speedway, Waltrip dominated the final 80 laps and took the checkered flag for the victory. He won again at the Pocono International Raceway.

One of six Luminas being campaigned on the NASCAR Winston Cup circuit, Waltrip's coupe, like its production counterpart, benefits from an advanced aerodynamic design that minimizes drag and amplifies stability. Chevy, in fact, designed the Lumina with racing in mind. NASCAR requires that the production coupe's styling lines be retained virtually intact for the race version. Despite being smaller than the Monte Carlo, the Lumina still "drafts" well, and in "slingshot" moves to the front of the pack, it breaks the air cleanly, making the move with ease.

While the production Lumina is a front-wheel drive car of unibody construction, the racing version has a thin metal shell of a body fitted to a custom-made, rear-drive chassis. To meet NASCAR regulations, the wheelbase is stretched from the street version's 107.5 inches to racing's 110 inches.

Lumina's overall body design enhances its aerodynamic balance, giving more stability and downforce in the front, and added downforce in the rear. On the racing machine, a front air dam lowers the nose to a scant three inches off the asphalt and adds downforce at the front of the car. Racers say the Lumina enters turns well and displays remarkable stability all the way from the apex of the corner to the straightaway. Properly set up, it handles well both in the high and low grooves of the straightway. Adapting to Waltrip's needs, Jeff Hammond and his crew change the steering ratios and weight balance, adjust the wheel camber, and make a variety of other adjustments on the car.

For example, downforce at each track is enhanced by a variety of rear spoilers, mandated by NASCAR to a maximum of 264 square inches. But teams have learned to adjust the angle of the rear spoiler according to the handling properties demanded by the various speedways. At the Michigan International Speedway, for instance, Waltrip's Hendrick Motorsports team angles the Lumina's rear spoiler at a steep 55 degrees. Michigan has big, sweeping corners with no discernable banking and the severe spoiler angle is needed to create rear-end downforce that helps keep the car on the track in the turns. By contrast, Daytona's steep banking requires a rear-spoiler angle of only 10 degrees. This gentle angle also makes the Lumina aerodynamically cleaner on the straightaways. That's an important factor at Daytona and Talledega, where NASCAR caps top speeds by requiring that carburetors be fitted with a plate that restricts the flow of fuel and limits horsepower.

Since the Lumina rides on a custom-built racing chassis, the team can tinker with the position of various components. Waltrip likes his car to go smoothly into turns with lots of grip all the way through. One way of accomplishing this is by locating the Lumina's tie rods and center links forward of the front spindle. This is called a front-steer setup. Some drivers prefer that the rear end of the car run somewhat loose in the corners, so they get a rear-steer setup, in which the tie rods and center links are placed aft of the front spindle. One benefit of front-steer is that the car can run a larger oil pan.

The Hendrick Lumina uses gas-filled shocks and a rear stabilizer bar similar to that of the production model. A truck arm with coil springs acts as the rear suspension.

Replacing the production powerplant — a 3.1 liter 60-degree V-6 engine with multi-port fuel injection — is the NASCAR-regulated 350-cubic-inch stock-block V-8 racing engine. It's bored out to a maximum of 358 cubic inches and is an adaptation of the 90-degree General Motors V-8. Bore ranges from 3.98 inches to 4.0. Rod length,

*While the production Lumina is a front-wheel drive car of unibody construction, the racing version (**left**) has a thin metal shell of a body fitted to a custom-made, rear-drive chassis. To meet NASCAR regulations, its wheelbase is stretched from the street version's 107.5 inches to 110. The overall body shape must remain virtually identical to the production car's.*

stroke, and cubic centimeters of volume in the aluminum heads vary from track to track. Compression ratios vary from 12.5:1 to 13.2:1.

The normally aspirated cast-iron small-block produces an average of 630 horsepower and 450 pounds/feet of torque. The block, cast aluminum heads, and internal components are sold over the counter, and can be found in Chevrolet's catalog. Installed in the aerodynamically slick Lumina, the engine provides better fuel mileage than it did in the Monte Carlo and allows more time between standard pit stops. The engine is capable of pushing the Lumina around superspeedways at more than 193 mph.

Inside the coupe, Waltrip's cockpit is fitted with a control to adjust the brake bias on the car. Where lots of braking is required, such as on the short tracks or at the triangular-shaped Pocono International Raceway, the control allows Waltrip to increase or reduce the front braking power.

Stock car drivers have always had guts. In the 1980s, they began to enjoy a bit of major-league glamour. And in 1985, they started to tussle for a glittering new prize, the Winston Million. This $1-million-dollar bonus is presented to any driver who, in a single season, wins three of NASCAR's four crown jewels: the Daytona 500, the richest race; the Winston 500 at Talledega, the fastest; the Coca Cola 600 at Charlotte Motor Speedway, the longest; and the Southern 500 at Darlington, the oldest. Bill Elliott is the only Winston Million winner so far, taking the competition's 1985 inaugural.

Waltrip clearly has his eyes on this prize. Beware the red bowtie, Bill. Darrell's dubbed his hot new Lumina the "Million-Dollar Race Car."

*Production-car interior is replaced with a no-nonsense racing setup (**opposite page, top left**), while the factory Lumina's V-6 is supplanted by a full-competition 358-cubic-inch V-8 capable of 630 horsepower (**opposite page, top right**). Chevy fans hope the Lumina (**opposite page, bottom, and above**) is a worthy heir to the winningest NASCAR stocker of all time, the 1979-'88 Monte Carlo.*

### Chevrolet Lumina NASCAR Coupe — Major Specifications

**Manufacturer:**

Laughlin Racing, Greenville, South Carolina/Hendrick Motorsports, Harrisburg, North Carolina

**Dimensions:**

| | |
|---|---|
| Wheelbase, in. | 110.0 |
| Overall length, in. | 198.3 |
| Overall width, in. | 71.5 |
| Overall height, in. | 50.5 |
| Track (front), in. | 60.5 |
| Track (rear), in. | 60.0 |
| Curb weight, lbs. | 3500 |

**Powertrain:**

| | |
|---|---|
| Layout: | front-engine, rear-wheel drive |
| Engine type: | overhead valve V-8 (aluminum heads) |
| Displacement, liters/cubic inches | NA/358 |
| Horsepower | 630 |
| Torque (lbs./ft.) | 450 |
| Fuel delivery: | 4-barrel carburetor |
| Transmission: | (oval tracks) 4-speed manual (road courses) Jerico 4-speed |

**Performance:**

| | |
|---|---|
| Top speed, mph | 193-plus |
| 0-60 mph, seconds | NA |
| Quarter-mile, seconds | NA |

| **Approximate Price:** | $75,000 |
|---|---|

# DE TOMASO PANTERA GT5-S

Who wouldn't be tempted by a mix of sizzling road performance and Italian style? Add the reliability of standard Detroit mechanical components, and the Pantera becomes a joy to behold, to drive, and to maintain. Unlike some high-priced sports cars, it doesn't demand the presence of a live-in engine specialist. In a time of high-tech gadgetry and fuel injection, the De Tomaso uses nothing more complex than a four-barrel Holley carburetor to meter its fuel intake.

The original Pantera of 1970 had a Ford engine and uncluttered Italian bodywork. The mid-mounted Ford V-8 survives, but De Tomaso has added wheel-arch flares, a tail wing, and various scoops and vents. The look is undeniably aggressive, perhaps exciting, if not altogether harmonious. Regardless, 350 horsepower and a 164-mph top end validate any claims made by the bellicose styling.

The combination of an Argentinian entrepreneur, Italian design, and Ford-USA marketing expertise sounds undeniably attractive. In fact, that's what inspired the birth of the De Tomaso Pantera, back in 1970. Four years later, Ford had lost interest in the project, production had collapsed, and the Pantera project seemed doomed. Not so. Fifteen years later the same car—modified and more powerful, but easily recognizable as a relative of the original—was still being built.

Inspiration for the project came from Alejandro de Tomaso, who had bought up several famous specialist businesses in Italy. In a complicated deal with Ford of Detroit (*not* Ford of Europe), he sold them the Ghia styling house. Ford then promised to provide engines for a new mid-engined supercar, and to sell it in America through the Lincoln-Mercury dealer chain.

The new mid-engined machine, named Pantera (Italian for "panther"), went into production in 1971. Its unitized body/chassis structure of pressed steel was built on the most rudimentary of tooling. Ford provided the big 351 cubic-inch (5.76-liter) "Cleveland" overhead-valve V-8 engine, which was mated to a West German ZF transmission. That gearbox style was also used the Ford GT40, the Maserati Bora, and other cars of this size and type.

"Standard 1960s Italian Supercar" could describe the rest of the chassis: all-independent coil-spring suspension, cast alloy wheels, big disc brakes, plus rack-and-pinion steering. The whole machine had a chunky yet purposeful character.

Tom Tjaarda, at Ghia in Turin, was responsible for the body design: a 2-seater closed coupe with a very sculptured look. The nose was wide and flat, with a wide windshield that sloped amply backward. Hinged metal covers hid the headlamps. Electric motors swiveled the covers upward for night driving.

Naturally, this was a *pure* 2-seater, with a big "systems" tunnel between the seats, and no stowage space up front. The spare tire took up most of the available trunk volume. Air conditioning was standard.

Behind the passengers sat the large, heavy, and simply engineered Ford V-8, which De Tomaso was willing to supply in a whole range of power outputs. To the rear of the engine, above the ZF transmission, a surprisingly useful luggage box made the Pantera more practical for long journeys than some of its compatriots.

The Pantera was intended to look visually exciting, to match what was being offered by Ferrari, Lamborghini, and Maserati. But under the sleek exterior it was meant to be mechanically more simple, so that the price could be kept down, and service problems in the U.S. would be minimized. In all these goals, it succeeded admirably.

Unfortunately, Pantera's humdrum mechanical birthright soon became widely known among motoring enthusiasts, some of whom expressed snobbishness about its origins. "Why," they wondered, "should we buy a car powered by the same cast-iron lump as we find in Galaxies and Thunderbirds?"

Ford-USA could probably have lived with that criticism if the early cars had been reliable. They were not. By 1974, with the energy crisis in full swing and with warranty costs soaring, Ford pulled out of the project after about 4,000 cars had been delivered.

De Tomaso, however, refused to abandon the Pantera. The rate of production was reduced, the system and location of assembly was simplified, but production carried on. For the rest of the 1970s and on into the 1980s, the Pantera remained on the market, looking much

A trio of GT5-S Panteras looks ready for takeoff (**left**). Pantera means "Panther" in Italian and the car does indeed exhibit cat-like reflexes, thanks to a responsive engine, wide tires, and a finely tuned suspension. The Pantera is a hybrid supercar: a European design powered by a 351-cubic-inch Ford "Cleveland" V-8 engine.

Strictly a 2-seater, Pantera's cabin of leather and wood (**above**) is a luxurious setting for fast driving. A brake-cooling duct is incorporated into the wide wheel-arch extension needed to clear the massive 35-section rear rubber (**left**). Pantera eschews fuel injection for good old-fashioned carburetion. This beautiful four-duce setup (**below**) is offered as one option on an engine that can be ordered with as little as 270 or as much as 350 horsepower. The GT5-S (**opposite page**) performs like a Ferrari, but requires less maintenance.

the same as before, still powered by the Ford V-8 engine, and still built with steel unibody construction.

Today, the top-of-the-line is the Pantera GT5-S, which has been facelifted considerably. It has a full-width, close-to-the-ground front spoiler and big wheelarch extensions. The suspension has wider-rimmed wheels and fatter tires than ever before: 285/40 section Pirellis on 10-inch rims at the front, 345/35 section on 13-inch rims at the rear. Pantera's original rugged good looks are still there, however, part angular and part rounded, with a big swallow-tail rear spoiler above the engine lid (Lamborghini Countach style). Equipment meets a very high standard, including air conditioning as well as leather-covered seats, doors, and fascia; power windows; central locking; and a long list of options.

On the road, it's still almost as rapid as anything being built at Maranello or Sant' Agata. You can order a GT5-S with 270, 300, or as much as 350 horsepower. With 300 horses under the hood, the GT5-S is capable of nearly 165 mph, and can certainly match Countach or Ferrari Testarossa acceleration up to the 100-mph mark. There is, after all, no substitute for torque (or as some would say, for cubic inches). The Cleveland engine offers a huge supply of both.

In fact, the Cleveland is an extremely flexible powerplant, which in De Tomaso form revs potently, up to 6,500 rpm in the intermediate gears. Its rather lumpy feel smoothes out above about 3,000 rpm, and the car seems to rush up to 140 mph and beyond. Third gear (of the five) is good for nearly 120 mph, and fourth for 145. Stability on winding roads is a strong point, a result in large measure of the enormous tires and accurately detailed suspension geometry. Despite the lack of power-assisted steering, it's an easy car to drive once on the move.

If only De Tomaso could convince the world that this is an extra-special Italian engine, and if only the company can make it sound less like a highly-tuned Corvette, success might reach greater heights.

## DeTomaso Pantera GT5 Major Specifications

**Manufacturer:**

De Tomaso Modena S.p.A.; Modena, Italy

**Dimensions:**

| | |
|---|---|
| Wheelbase, in. | 98.8 |
| Overall length, in. | 168.1 |
| Overall width, in. | 77.6 |
| Overall height, in. | 43.3 |
| Track (front), in. | 59.4 |
| Track (rear), in. | 62.2 |
| Curb weight, lbs. | 3268 |

**Powertrain:**

| | |
|---|---|
| Layout: | mid-engine, rear-wheel drive |
| Engine type: | overhead-valve V-8 |
| Displacement, liters/cubic inches | 5.8/351 |
| Horsepower @ rpm | 350 @ 6000 |
| Torque (lbs./ft.) @ rpm | 333 @ 3800 |
| Fuel delivery: | Holley 4-barrel carburetor |
| Transmission: | 5-speed ZF manual |

**Performance:**

| | |
|---|---|
| Top speed, mph | 164 |
| 0-60 mph, seconds | est. 5.5 |
| Quarter-mile, seconds | est. 14.0 |

| **Approximate price:** | **$55,000** |
|---|---|

# DODGE/SHELBY VIPER R/T10

**V**isitors to the North American International Auto Show in Detroit in January 1989 stood transfixed at the sight of Dodge's offering in the concept-car arena. Anyone familiar with Carroll Shelby's AC-Cobras of the 1960s could hardly help but be drawn backward in time—to a time of fewer worldly worries, with muscular motors and sports cars that looked tough and ready for a heavy foot. And if a V-8 was the biggest powerplant available in those days, this Dodge/Shelby creation of 1989 carried a V-10! Chrysler pledges that the Viper will go into production, probably as a 1992 model. It's likely to offer both a 300-horsepower V-8 and the V-10.

Viper history, and its Shelby connection, reach back several years. The "futurethink" Lamborghini Portofino, a Chrysler/Lamborghini joint effort, was a superb execution in a 4-passenger car that looked as if it had arrived from another galaxy. During 1986, designer Kevin Verduyn penned the Navajo at Chrysler's Pacifica styling studio in California, a car conjured up as an exotic 4-door for a possible mid-90s product. When Chrysler acquired Lamborghini a year later, the idea of fitting the Navajo onto an existing Lambo caught on and led to modification of a mid-engine Jalpa. The mid-section of the Jalpa was stretched by 26 inches and the workings went into place

as the origin of another car, this one with inspiration to become a real automobile. After Lamborghini added doors modeled after the Countach and sweeping exterior lines to visibly continue the Lamborghini lineage, the new Portofino was born.

Once the purchase of Lamborghini was complete, an exchange program between Highland Park, Michigan and Turin, Italy settled the Portofino issue: The car would be moved to Coggiola in Turin for fabrication. Four months later, a complete car rolled out for all the world to see during the Frankfurt Auto Show. The staid Chrysler Corporation, with a reputation for making every car in its universe an uninspired, boxy people-mover powered by a 2.2-liter engine, suddenly pulsed with new life. The Portofino was dazzling by any standard; and since it was a rather conventional and well-developed Jalpa underneath, it was that much closer to becoming reality as a showroom model, with an actual price sticker on the window.

Imagine tooling into your driveway in an ultra-space-age Buck Rogers machine. Then imagine your neighbor's reaction as you press the latches on what was once a B-pillar location: Guillotine doors rise upward to completely open the side of the car, exposing a luxurious, deep leathered interior that invites you to step into another world.

Brawny, bold, and brutally styled, the Viper concept car (**both pages**) is an unashamed throwback to the Shelby AC-Cobra roadsters of the 1960s. It even sports a serpent-inspired name, just like its spiritual predecessor. The R/T10's exaggerated hood and short deck celebrate its classic front-engine, rear-drive, 2-seat configuration. The car has the same 96.2-inch wheelbase as the Corvette, but is 4.5-inches shorter overall. Chrysler is seriously contemplating its production.

Portofino would have been the kind of car that might change your life—and it came tantalizingly close to reality.

Instead, picture this scenario. The combination of Chrysler and Lamborghini takes that tempting but fallen Portofino, moves the cockpit back, and chops out the second seat to make a 2-seater. Next they snip the top to turn it into a Targa-style roadster, add sinfully sensuous curves here and there to create a voluptuous aluminum body, mount the widest tires imaginable all around, drop a powerful V-10 engine up front, and install a set of tubular exhausts that would make a pipe organist quiver with envy. Slap the name "Viper" on the sides and *voila!*—another sports car that could change your life.

The Viper RT/10 is that car. Or will be, if it ever reaches the marketplace. If anything has come along that's reminiscent of the old 427 Cobra, this is the culprit. And guess what? The inimitable Carroll Shelby—creator of that muscular attack craft of a quarter-century ago—has lent a hand to this one, too. Back in the early 1960s, Shelby (with help from Ford) molded his chicken-farmer turned sports-car-racer talents into a roadster that shook the world of automobiles. Will it happen again?

Those names suggest it might. Cobra—hisses. Viper—hisses. But surprisingly, the new name came from the Chrysler chiefs close to the project, not from Mr. Shelby. They see the Viper as a way to implement the first phases of some of Chrysler's plans for the future, not as a platform for the world's fastest sports car. In the end, they just might have it both ways.

Like the Cobra and a host of other sportsters of the muscular past, the Viper is front engine/rear drive. A throwback? Absolutely. But one that's worked so well in times past—and can still excite the passion of driving. If all goes well, that passion could be traveling 0-100 mph at a faster pace than anything volume-produced today.

Penned by Pacifica stylists, the Viper is the brainchild of a few Chrysler Motors insiders, beginning with Bob Lutz, the company president and a motorsports enthusiast. It starts with Chrysler's concept of a powerful, fuel-injected V-10 engine for a line of high-performance trucks—the sort that might pull expensive boats and horse trailers rather than haul humdrum cargo. That's how the corporation can justify such a radical break away from the zillions of 2.2-liter fours that are still plying the highways of America.

The V-10 offers the same sort of advantages that a V-12 holds over a V-8: smaller piston area and reduced combustion-chamber volume for improved combustion, giving more complete fuel burning and increased efficiency, thus improved economy. Higher rpm capability is a natural for a sports car, but the Viper's engine measures 8-liters! Compare that to the less than 5-liters displaced by Ferrari's flat 12.

Trucking needs torque, of course, and torque comes from cubic inches. The RT/10 measures a whopping 488 cubes. No apologies, thank you, just brutal pulling power in the Viper's lightweight application. The engine's over-square 4.0-inch bore and 3.88-inch stroke suggest that the V-10 will be a quick winder able to put out over 300 horsepower, slamming hard with upwards of 500 pound/feet of neck-snapping torque.

Sure, it has more internal parts than a V-8, and more contact surface area to produce more friction. Still, loads are distributed better and stress is lower, so parts can be lighter. Using modern thin-wall casting techniques, that makes the RT/10 more than competitive when comparing its weight to today's V-8. Light alloys help reduce overall weight, and high-tech thermoplastic parts are entering the production process. Although the engine has an odd firing sequence (because of the 10 cylinders), having more pulses than an eight implies smoother overall performance. Being a "conventional" V-10 means that exotic valve and cam designs have been discarded in favor of proven hardware for long-lived simplicity.

To get it right from the beginning, the cast-iron engine started with a clean slate. Unlike early proposals, it's not a V-8 with two more cylinders tacked on. Aluminum blocks may be on the way. Looking into the future, lopping off two cylinders (or four) from a V-10 would make a smaller-displacement V-8, and still smaller V-6, both smooth firing. Sounds as though Chrysler's engine people have been thinking cleverly about corporate products for the 1990s.

Whether in V-8 or V-10 form, the Viper is certain to be a stellar performer, an instant collectable, and a dynamite image car for Chrysler Motors. Credit the automaker with the guts to stay true to the prototype. When Chrysler Chairman Lee Iacocca gave the Viper project the green light his instructions to engineers and designers were the same any hot-blooded enthusiast might utter. Said Iacocca, "Keep it a hero."

*Viper has a bullet-like profile (**opposite page, top**). Its interior (**opposite page, bottom**) carries over the traditional sports-car theme, with simple analog gauges, drilled pedals, and leather bucket seats. Derived from a proposed Chrysler truck engine, the V-10 (**this page**) displaces a whopping 8 liters. With an estimated 300-plus horsepower and enormous torque, it should be capable of race-car like acceleration and a 160-mph top end.*

### Dodge/Shelby Viper R/T10 Major Specifications

**Manufacturer:**
Dodge Division of Chrysler Motors; Highland Park, Michigan.
Concept car built in Newport Beach, California

**Dimensions:**

| | |
|---|---|
| Wheelbase, in. | 96.2 |
| Overall length, in. | 172.0 |
| Overall width, in. | 75.6 |
| Overall height, in. | 46.2 |
| Track (front), in. | 59.6 |
| Track (rear), in. | 60.8 |
| Curb weight, lbs. | NA |

**Powertrain:**

| | |
|---|---|
| Layout: | front-engine, rear-wheel drive |
| Engine type: | overhead-valve V-10 |
| Displacement, liters/cubic inches | 8.0/488 |
| Horsepower @ rpm | 300-plus @ NA |
| Torque (lbs./ft.) @ rpm | 450 @ NA |
| Fuel delivery: | multi-point fuel injection |
| Transmission: | 5-speed manual |

**Performance:**

| | |
|---|---|
| Top speed, mph | NA |
| 0-60 mph, seconds | NA |
| Quarter-mile, seconds | NA |
| **Approximate price:** | NA |

# FERRARI
# F40

Introduced in 1987 to celebrate the 40th anniversary
of Enzo Ferrari as an automaker, the F40 (**both pages**)
consciously minimizes its use of high-technology in
favor of a vital rawness that helped make Ferraris
legends in the first place.

originally intended for motorsport. This was the car from which the F40 was directly developed. The basis of the design was a sturdy multi-tubular steel chassis frame, strengthened by Kevlar, while the bodywork was made of carbon fiber or Kevlar. After learning about the materials to be used, everyone suddenly understood why the price had to be so high. Because of this construction, and the race-proven design methods used, the curb weight was kept down to 2,425 pounds.

As with the GTO *Evoluzione*, the engine is a twin-turbocharged version of the classic 4-cam, 4-valve V-8 which, in less highly tuned form, was fitted to the 328 GTB/GTS road cars. Although it displaces only 179 cubic inches (2,936 cc), it pushes out no less than 480 horsepower. Ferrari was also willing to supply F40s with larger turbochargers, different cam profiles, and an extra 200 horsepower!

The rest of the chassis is familiar to those Ferrari-lovers who had already drooled over the 288 GTO. Details include a coil-spring all-independent suspension and massive ventilated disc brakes all around. The engine drives through a twin-plate clutch, 5-speed all-synchromesh gearbox, and limited-slip differential. Ferrari made a "dog" gearbox available for competition use.

Three different suspension settings can be chosen from the mountings and the Koni adjustable dampers: normal, high-speed (which lowers the car by 0.8 inch), and "parking," where the suspension can be raised by the same amount. Naturally, for a car of this weight, there is no power assist for either the brakes or the rack-and-pinion steering.

Bodywork is at once starkly trimmed and finished, yet with some odd luxuries. The side windows, for instance, have to be slid sideways to open, rather than wound up and down or operated by small electric motors. The seats are rock hard, but are figure-hugging, competition "buckets" offered in various sizes to suit customers' figures. Four-point safety harnesses are provided and full air

A rear wing and strategic body venting control air flow over and through the F40 (**below**). Its aft section hinges to provide access to the longitudinally mounted twin-turbo V-8 (**opposite page**). Feather-weight materials in the body and frame keep the F40 to a svelte 2425 pounds.

A vented plastic cover aids engine-compartment air flow (**below**). Competition-style F40 seats (**bottom**) are form-fitted to the owner's body, then secured to the car's frame. Running fast and free (**right**), the F40 is the essence of Ferrari, even if purists scoff that it lacks a 12-cylinder engine. A sparkling 2.9-liter V-8 ensures credibility with 478 horsepower and a top speed of 200 mph.

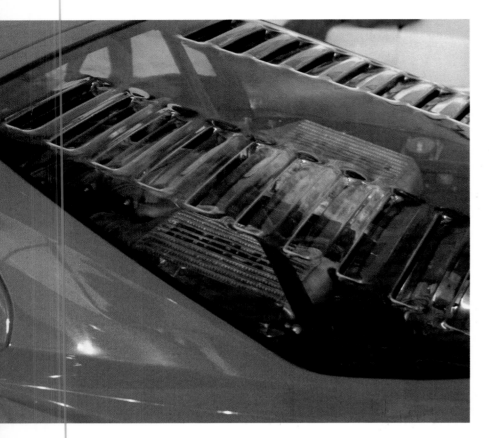

conditioning is standard.

Style is both luscious and functional. The nose is wide and low, both headlamps hidden behind perspex covers. Only a single wiper sweeps across the wide, well-angled windshield.

Although Pininfarina claims to have carried out extensive wind-tunnel development work, intakes and exit slots seem to be almost everywhere. Apart from narrow but full-width intakes in the nose, two NACA ducts stand ahead of the windshield to feed the air conditioning. Hot air, having passed through the front radiator, is expelled through big vertical slots behind the front wheels.

More NACA ducts low down on the flanks lead air to the rear brakes, while conventional scoops (whose profiles begin on the door skins themselves) feed air into the engine bay. That isn't all. Above and behind the rear wheels are two more NACA ducts also feeding the engine bay, along with a series of louvers in the rear quarters, behind the wheels.

A fantastic creation the F40 is, whether for motoring on the open road or, perhaps, for use in motor racing, where the regulations are in its favor. Except for the fact that Ferrari equipped the F40 with enough creature comforts to lure any reluctant buyers, it is no more or less than a reined-in race car. No bumpers are available to help fend off kamikaze Chevrolets in the rush hour. Out back, there is no sensible luggage space for packing a tux and an evening gown or two. Most emphatically, there are no deep-pile carpets or complex radio installations to keep driver or passengers amused. To get at the engine bay, you have to lift the whole of the rear bodywork. Not only is there no hydraulic assistance, but a prop is needed to keep everything open.

The F40, in other words, is meant to be driven fast. Very fast—with no concessions made to anything less. The ultra-wide Pirelli tires (335/35ZR17 at the rear) are there to grip tightly and respond capably, not to deliver any sort of refinement or sound-absorbing qualities. Not even a Porsche 959 owner is likely to get away—and that's precisely what Ferrari fanciers want from their motorcars.

## Ferrari F40 Major Specifications

**Manufacturer:**

Ferrari S.p.A.; Modena, Italy

**Dimensions:**

| | |
|---|---:|
| Wheelbase, in. | 96.5 |
| Overall length, in. | 174.4 |
| Overall width, in. | 78.0 |
| Overall height, in. | 44.5 |
| Track (front), in. | 62.8 |
| Track (rear), in. | 63.4 |
| Curb weight, lbs. | 2425 |

**Powertrain:**

| | |
|---|---:|
| Layout: | mid-engine, rear-wheel drive |
| Engine type: | twin-turbocharged double-overhead-cam V-8 |
| Displacement, liters/cubic inches | 2.9/179 |
| Horsepower @ rpm | 478 @ 7000 |
| Torque (lbs./ft.) @ rpm | 425 @ 4000 |
| Fuel delivery: | Weber-Marelli multi-point fuel injection |
| Transmission: | 5-speed manual |

**Performance:**

| | |
|---|---:|
| Top speed, mph | 201 |
| 0-60 mph, seconds | est. 4.1 |
| Quarter-mile, seconds | 11.9 |

| | |
|---|---:|
| **Approximate price:** | $250,000 |

# FERRARI GTO

Introduced in 1984, the GTO (**below**) revives a hallowed Ferrari name. The letters stand for Gran Turismo Omologato, meaning a grand touring car that has been approved, or homologated, for racing. The European competition class for which the GTO was originally intended dissolved before the Ferrari could participate, but its race-bred manners survive to terrorize lesser road cars.

oth on the race course and the open road, the Italian automakers seldom skimp on style—or on speed. The very names of their supercars cause an enthusiast's heart to start thumping in anticipation—or envy, once the price tag for this brand of excitement is noted.

Names seldom tell all, of course. Yet you only have to translate the initials "GTO" from the Italian to predict the hard-breathing nature of this example from the near-mythical Ferrari motorworks. GTO stands for *Gran Turismo Omologato*. That means it is a car produced in sufficient numbers to allow it to be used in suitable motorsport events. Unstated (but understood) is the fact that it also carries a motor-racing pedigree.

This recent edition wasn't the first Ferrari GTO, but the second. The original, produced in the 1960s, was a front-engine 2-seater powered by a 3-liter V-12. A hard act to follow, but the 1980s variety was actually much faster, more sophisticated—and more numerous on the road.

The basic story of this layout really begins with the famous Dino 246 GT of 1969-1973. That one had a simple but rigid all-independently sprung chassis, a transversely mounted V-6 engine behind the seats (driving the rear wheels), and was topped off by a beautiful Pininfarina body style.

Next came the 308 GTB of 1975, which used the same chassis, but originally had a transverse-mounted 179 cubic-inch (2.9-liter), 4-cam, 90-degree V-8 engine—and yet another magnificent Pininfarina shape. In the 1980s this model became the 328 GTB, powered by a 3.2-liter

engine with 4 valves per cylinder. An open-top "Spyder" version gained the most popularity, soon becoming the belle of the motor-car ball.

Seen first at the Geneva Motor Show in March 1984, the GTO is a much-developed version of the 308 GTB layout, but much more powerful and technically more advanced. Even though 4-wheel-drive had become fashionable by this time, the GTO is rear-wheel drive.

Though slightly longer in wheelbase than the current 328 GTB, the GTO displays very similar chassis engineering and the same basic "family" styling lines. It was built only as a mid-engine, 2-seater closed coupe. The engine, however, is realigned, with its crankshaft along the line of the chassis, rather than transverse. Behind it stands a new gearbox/final-drive transmission.

Although it's fully equipped for road use, Ferrari had originally

*The GTO's flowing body (**above, and opposite page, top**) is based upon the mid-engine design first seen on Dinos in the late 1960s and revamped for the V-8 308 series in the mid-'70s. It's longer than the 308 to accommodate a longitudinally mounted engine. The leather-lined cabin (**right**) is classic Ferrari, replete with prancing-horse insignia and bright-metal gear-shift gate.*

conceived the car for racing, and for running in high-speed tarmac rallies. When it was launched, Ferrari stated that exactly 200 cars would be built, the minimum required to gain Group B racing approval.

The sporting requirement meant that the same basic engine as used in the 328 GTB was slightly reduced in size, to 174 cubic inches (2,855 cc). At the same time, it was equipped with twin Japanese-made IHI turbochargers, one for each bank of cylinders. Naturally, there is an air-to-air intercooler close to each turbocharger. That combination gives the standard-specification GTO no less than 400 horsepower, churned out at an ear-popping 7,000 rpm.

In body style, the GTO looks rather like the existing 328 GTB, though it is a wider and more specialized car. Pininfarina carried forward one of its styling "signatures" from the 328 GTB: the air scoops whose profiles indent the top of the passenger doors and feed air into the engine bay ahead of the rear wheels. All of the cars, naturally, are painted in Ferrari red. What other color could possibly do justice to the job?

In standard form, the body was crafted mainly of steel. As usual, it took shape in the Ferrari-owned body factory in Modena itself. Actually, a number of fiberglass—and even advanced composite, or honeycomb—materials were used. The GTO, in other words, draws heavily on the expertise gained by Ferrari in Formula 1 single-seater racing back in the early 1980s.

As it happens, Ferrari remained bound up in its single-seat program. That left the GTO out in the cold, and it was never used in motorsport.

By the end of the run, no fewer than 271 cars were produced. An even fiercer "Evoluzione" version (of which 20 cars had to be made to gain sporting approval) had been proposed, but this project never got off the ground.

Even before production ceased, the GTO had become an instant collector's item. How could it not, since it is a superb road car with magnificent performance and handling? In Ferrari terms, it has everything: performance, charisma, glamor and breeding.

Here is a dedicated "Supercar" for the rich connoisseur, one which at the time ranked as the fastest Ferrari road car yet. It is, after all, more powerful, but lighter and smaller, than the fabled Boxer; more nimble and with better aerodynamics than the also-new Testarossa.

No GTO driver is likely to be outrun by any other current road car. Even the latest Lamborghini Countach Quattrovalvole would have to struggle to match the GTO's pace. Only when Porsche's technical *tour-de-force*, the 959, finally went on sale did the GTO have to stand aside.

Like several other limited-production machines, many GTOs were purchased by speculators, then instantly stored away as automotive investments to await the inevitable rise in value. That might make sense economically, but means that few buyers ever experience anything close to the GTO's top speed—nearly 190 mph. No public road can provide an opportunity to verify this claim, of course. But the car's other attributes, easier to test, are no less thrilling. Investment-minded buyers seldom feel its flashing acceleration, race-proved steering, roadholding, and general behavior. It's certainly the closest thing to a pure-bred racing sports car that any mortal is likely to drive on the open road.

No car, of course, is unbeatable. Ferrari soon set out to prove that by competing against itself. By 1987, the much more specialized F40, created to celebrate the marque's 40th anniversary in the car-building business, had been announced. It would boast even higher performance giving more race-minded (and affluent) motorists a chance to experience the excitement of driving a legend.

A limited production of just 271 GTOs helps make the car an object of wealthy collectors, but its racer-like roadholding and out-of-this world acceleration are what enthrall the true driving enthusiast. The car's official name is the 288 GTO, denoting its 2855-cc engine of 8 cylinders. The previous GTO was the 250 GTO of 1962, a front-engine sports-racer powered by a 3-liter V-12. At that time, Enzo Ferrari used a different displacement-related calculation to name his cars.

## Ferrari GTO Major Specifications

**Manufacturer:**

Ferrari S.p.A.; Modena, Italy

**Dimensions:**

| | |
|---|---|
| Wheelbase, in. | 96.5 |
| Overall length, in. | 168.9 |
| Overall width, in. | 75.2 |
| Overall height, in. | 44.1 |
| Track (front), in. | 62.5 |
| Track (rear), in. | 61.5 |
| Curb weight, lbs. | 2557 |

**Powertrain:**

| | |
|---|---|
| Layout: | mid-engine, rear-wheel drive |
| Engine type: | twin turbocharged double-overhead-cam V-8 |
| Displacement, liters/cubic inches | 2.9/174 |
| Horsepower @ rpm | 394 @ 7000 |
| Torque (lbs./ft.) @ rpm | 366 @ 3800 |
| Fuel delivery: | Weber-Marelli fuel injection |
| Transmission: | 5-speed manual |

**Performance:**

| | |
|---|---|
| Top speed, mph | 190 |
| 0-60 mph, seconds | est. 4.9 |
| Quarter-mile, seconds | 12.7 |

| | |
|---|---|
| **Approximate price:** | $125,000 |

# FERRARI
# TESTAROSSA

**A** mere glance at the Testarossa's rakish red profile is enough to set a young (or not so young) driver's heart to throbbing. Slip down inside and stomp on the gas, and that heart just might come dangerously close to stopping—at least for a moment. Here is Ferrari at its finest: sleek, swift, and special, carrying on the legendary family's name and reputation into the 1990s.

Combine *three* famous names—Ferrari, Pininfarina, and Testarossa—and it's easy to see why this mid-engine Italian Supercar couldn't

Ferrari's signature supercar, the take-no-prisoners Testarossa (**below**). A 5.0-liter flat-12 powers the Pininfarina-penned exotic to more than 175 mph. Testarossa's huge side vents use "cheese-slicer" grille work to stay within European laws limiting air-intake sizes. Originally derided by some critics, the grilles have become a Testarossa trademark and a widely copied styling feature.

help but build its own fan club in a hurry. Any Ferrari, after all, evokes tormented cravings among knowledgeable sports-car aficionados. Set a sensational body style atop a modern mid-engine chassis, and this one was bound to become a best-seller.

Still puzzled by the mystique? Then just contemplate the road potential of this 170-mph bomb, whose flat 12-cylinder engine makes wonderfully authentic race-car noises, and which offers acceleration and roadability to match the enticing sounds. Sure, it's impractical for everyday travel, with very little storage space and what might charitably be called a magisterial turning circle. Yet none of that matters. Above all, the Testarossa is fast. Extremely fast. And that alone was quite enough to cause lines to form at the dealerships when the car first appeared. In fact, many customers were happy to pay a premium price to make sure they took delivery early.

The story of this car really starts with the 365 GT4 Berlinetta Boxer of the 1970s, the second mid-engine road car design to be put on sale by the famous Italian manufacturer. (The V-6 Dino had been the first.) Like all such Ferraris of the period, the Boxer had a rugged multi-tube chassis frame, with coil-spring independent suspension all around. Pininfarina created a sleekly-rounded 2-seater coupe body, which looked very similar indeed to the mid-engine 308/328 GTB that followed a few years later.

A newly-developed four-cam flat-12 engine was mounted behind the 2-seater cabin. But because the 5-speed gearbox also stood ahead of the rear wheels, the engine actually sat on top of the transmission— and above the final drive itself. At first, a 268-cubic-inch (4.4-liter) engine supplied the power. Later in the 1970s it grew to 302 cubic inches (4,942 cc). Eventually, with Bosch fuel injection added, this 160-mph-plus car became known as the 512i BB.

The "Boxer," as it was always called by Ferrari fans (who number in the millions, even if only a handful could ever afford to buy one), always *looked* faster than it was. In fact, the manufacturer's claims were never substantiated by independent tests. Not only that, but the Boxer's style lacked some of the eye-catching qualities of its head-to-head rival, the Lamborghini Countach. So when the time came for a replacement, the new Ferrari not only had to look different; it had to be just as aerodynamically efficient *and* more powerful.

Ferrari launched its Boxer replacement in Europe in the autumn of 1984, and chose to call it Testarossa. The reason was simple: The cylinder-head covers of the engine were painted red (like another famous racing Ferrari of the 1950s). *Testarossa*, of course, sounds a lot more romantic in Italian than it ever could in the English language. The translation, depressingly prosaic for such a spectacular motorcar, is simply "Red Head."

Because Pininfarina had produced a startlingly attractive body style, the Testarossa looked like an all-new model. Yet under the skin are a chassis and running gear based on the long-lived Boxer. The same multi-tube chassis stands on a 100.4-inch wheelbase, with rack-and-pinion steering, all-independent rear suspension, and four-wheel disc brakes. The twin cooling radiators are relocated, however, one to each side of the engine bay. Wider wheels and tires help the car show off its supercar roadholding skills.

Purists weren't pleased to see that the new model retained the same basic Boxer engine/transmission layout. Once again, they complained that the engine was too high, and that on-the-limit roadholding was therefore impaired. Though similar in configuration to its predecessor, the 302-cubic-inch powerplant was reworked by Ferrari engineers. New 4-valve-per-cylinder heads result in a rated output of 390 horsepower at 6300 rpm, with an even more impressive torque spread than before.

Pininfarina's body design is a squat, very wide-hipped (78 inches) 2-seater coupe, with rear-view mirrors that stick out even farther. Heavily staked and finned flanks on the bodysides aren't there just for show; they lead air into the radiator cooling ducts. The nose is almost "standard Ferrari," with pop-up headlamps; but the tail end carries more horizontal stripes, to emphasize the sheer bulk of the car.

Ferrari will happily make a right-hand-drive Testarossa (**opposite page**) for its British, Australian, and Japanese customers. The car is an astonishing 77.8-inches wide—virtually the same as a Porsche 962 race car—and its 65.4-inch rear track (**below**) is two inches broader even than a Lamborghini Countach's. The width contributes to both the Testarossa's handling and its legend.

Crimson cylinder-head covers on the car's horizontally opposed 12-cylinder (**below**) give currency to the literal meaning of Testarossa: "red head." The original 1950s Testa Rossa was a full race car. Interior accommodations (**bottom**) are luxurious and sporting. Ferrari takes pains to improve cabin comfort by locating the radiators behind the passenger compartment, in the car's flanks, so boiling coolant won't have to be routed past the driver and passenger.

The Testarossa might not be the fastest car in the world. That honor was probably first held by the Porsche 959, then by the Ferrari F40 in 1987. Even so, the Testarossa certainly *looks* as if it were doing 100 mph even when relaxing in a parking lot.

The sheer size of the car—along with all the slots, intakes, and ducting—must have had an effect on the aerodynamics because the true top speed falls below 180 mph. On the other hand, a sprint away from a traffic light rockets the car past the 100-mph mark in a mere 11.4 seconds—assuming, of course, that no black-and-white stands ready to call a halt to such a blazing (and blatantly illegal) surge of speed.

To get this kind of acceleration, you drop the clutch at about 4500 rpm in first gear, slam through the gears as quickly as possible, but don't even hit fourth gear (of the five) until the speedometer nudges 100 mph. First gear, incidentally, is good for 50 mph at 6800 rpm.

Although it is certainly possible to drive a Testarossa slowly—and to be fair to Ferrari's engineers, the car is quite docile in heavy traffic—it truly shines when in its hustling mode. Until you reach the limits of its handling powers, everything is well-balanced and reassuring; but the nose might run out in tight corners on wet roads, while an oversteering slide is always possible when booting the baby out of the same turn in a lower gear.

Although the Testarossa looks like a racing car and sounds like a racing car, it's decked out with many—though hardly all—of the common comforts of the road. Air conditioning and leather upholstery come standard. The gear lever operates within a visible "gate," without which no Ferrari would look complete. Testing a Testarossa for *Road & Track*, Paul Frere warned that this was "still a he-man's car," partly because of its reluctant gearshift.

The only other caveat?—that the lucky man or woman eager to climb behind the wheel carries a well-filled pocketbook to pay for the pleasure of this redhead's company.

## Ferrari Testarossa Major Specifications

**Manufacturer:**

Ferrari S.p.A.; Modena, Italy

**Dimensions:**

| | |
|---|---|
| Wheelbase, in. | 100.4 |
| Overall length, in. | 176.6 |
| Overall width, in. | 77.8 |
| Overall height, in. | 44.5 |
| Track (front), in. | 59.8 |
| Track (rear), in. | 65.4 |
| Curb weight, lbs. | 3660 |

**Powertrain:**

| | |
|---|---|
| Layout: | mid-engine, rear-wheel drive |
| Engine type: double overhead-cam horizontally opposed 12-cylinder | |
| Displacement, liters/cubic inches | 4.9/301 |
| Horsepower @ rpm | 380 @ 5750 |
| Torque (lbs./ft.) @ rpm | 354 @ 4500 |
| Fuel delivery: | twin multi-point fuel injection |
| Transmission: | 5-speed manual |

**Performance:**

| | |
|---|---|
| Top speed, mph | 177.7 |
| 0-60 mph, seconds | est. 5.8 |
| Quarter-mile, seconds | 13.8 |

| | |
|---|---|
| **Approximate price:** | $140,780 |

# KOENIG COMPETITION FERRARI TESTAROSSA

**W**hen is the 178-mph top speed of a stock Testarossa not enough? Only when it's possible to squeeze out a little more, naturally. Or a *lot* more, even nearing the 225-mph mark.

Perhaps Willy Koenig, the West German auto tuner, has never heard the phrase "gilding the lily." Then again, perhaps he has, but doesn't care. As far as most normal mortals are concerned, reworking the famed Italian Ferrari Testarossa amounts to tampering with near-perfection. Such an act might even verge on sacrilege. Koenig does not agree, and the "Koenig Competition" is the result. Radically revised in both mechanics and appearance, with performance that pushes well beyond the ordinary Ferrari limits, the Koenig conversion is a very rare car and, because of its extrovert nature, is likely to remain so.

Willy Koenig operates from Munich, where his workshops specialize in super-tuning cars like the Testarossa and the Lamborghini Countach. Only rich customers need apply, for his work usually doubles the car's original asking price. Koenig's conversions are complete, embracing everything from engine work to bodywork changes. Needless to say, his efforts are neither requested nor approved by the car makers themselves.

Most of us might consider the "plain" Testarossa, with its standard 390 horsepower and top speed of around 180 mph, to be quite quick enough—especially at the price asked. A few people— doubtless a *very* few people, for Koenig has asked about $350,000 for each of his creations—have been happy to buy a much-changed Testarossa. As modified, the engine is boosted to a claimed 800 horsepower, ready to deliver a top speed approaching 225 mph. Compared with the basic Ferrari, Koenig's creation looks more dramatic, but certainly

From the kitchens of Willy Koenig comes a cookin' Testarossa (**both pages**). The recipe for this brand of rapid transit: Take one 12-cylinder Ferrari, add two turbochargers and a supercharger. Trim off all the stock body panels except the roof and the windshield. Add lightweight, custom-designed replacement panels and new seats. Revamp the instrumentation. Let simmer on any street until a crowd gathers. Then turn up the heat on a sizzling 800 horsepower. Don't forget to add plenty of dough: about $400,000.

less "pure." It's also noisier, and comes closer to race-car status than the original.

Except for the original roof panel and windshield, Koenig ditched the rest of the Testarossa's bodywork, substituting a new set of carbon-Kevlar panels. Headlamps are visible behind clear plastic covers. Twin turbos *and* a supercharger combine to squeeze the utmost fuel and air into the engine when duty calls, while the injection systems get new settings. The basic fabric has been left alone; likewise the gearbox and chassis. Tires are even wider than standard; after all, with up to 800 horsepower available, the rears have to be very wide and grippy. So 335-section Pirelli P Zeros run on 17-inch alloy rims from the OZ wheel company.

Willy Koenig himself claimed that the Competition was a lot faster than any other car in the world, and he was adamant that it could easily outpace a Ferrari F40. Koenig further insisted that the F40 was not a luxury car, whereas his monstrous creation was for customers "who want luxury in a road car that resembles a Group C car—a car that you can drive very slowly, or very fast." Checking out his claims was no easy matter, of course, even on a test track. After all, few cars could reach such phenomenal velocities without taking off, and most needed several miles of straight and level track to reach those speeds.

On the move, a Koenig feels just like the monster promised by the specifications. One instinctively feels that here is a car designed for use on cool, still days over a dry road. Gusty conditions, especially on wet and slippery surfaces, are enough to make ordinary drivers (as opposed to the Ayrton Sennas or Alain Prosts of this world) rather cautious.

Koenig's Testarossa (**opposite page**) dispenses with the factory Ferrari's pop-up headlamps so as not to sacrifice any speed from its claimed top end near 200 mph. Getting the power to the ground are massive 13-inch wide tires on 17-inch diameter wheels (**below**). The stock Ferrari gets by on 16-inch wheels shod with 9.4-inch-wide tires in front and 11-inch-wide rubber in the rear.

Not only is it a very powerful car—probably the most powerful car ever seen on the public highway—but it's also a very noisy machine. When fired up, the engine tends to idle at nearly 2000 rpm, whirring and humming and shooting vibrations into the less-than-rigid bodywork.

To get a Koenig underway involves expert work with the clutch, but the engine is surprisingly flexible—if never quiet during any of its exertions. When the twin turbos finally chime in at about 3500 rpm, the engine bay erupts in a cacophony of sound that makes conversation impossible—assuming that the driver isn't already too preoccupied to chat. The engine always feels amazingly smooth, but hard and competition-tuned.

Can the Koenig truly beat 220 mph? No tester seems to have found out for sure, but the chassis, the huge competition-style brakes, and the well-balanced handling have all proved themselves. At very high speeds the Koenig is a car that whistles and bellows, dumping its turbocharger boost with a flutter if you lift your right foot, and stepping over the handling limit with a lurch if you get it wrong.

Exciting? You bet. Practical? No way. But then, if you can afford a car like the Koenig, the practical side of things doesn't enter into the equation, anyway.

Koenig upgrades the Testarossa's seating with competition-style buckets and changes the instrumentation from orange on black to black on red (**above**). The 4.9-liter Boxer twelve (**opposite page, top**) gets two turbochargers, a supercharger, two intercoolers, and internal modifications. Oil and coolant capacity are increased 50 percent, as well. Aerodynamics govern styling revamp (**right**).

## Koenig Ferrari Testarossa Major Specifications

**Manufacturer:**

Koenig Specials GmbH; Munich, West Germany

**Dimensions:**

| | |
|---|---:|
| Wheelbase, in. | 100.4 |
| Overall length, in. | 178.4 |
| Overall width, in. | 85.0 |
| Overall height, in. | 44.9 |
| Track (front), in. | NA |
| Track (rear), in. | NA |
| Curb weight, lbs. | 3750 |

**Powertrain:**

| | |
|---|---:|
| Layout: | mid-engine, rear-wheel drive |
| Engine type: | twin turbocharged, supercharged, intercooled, horizontally opposed 12-cylinder |
| Displacement, liters/cubic inches | 4.9/302 |
| Horsepower @ rpm | 789 @ 6500 |
| Torque (lbs./ft.) @ rpm | 664 @ 5000 |
| Fuel delivery: | Bosch KE-Jetronic fuel injection |
| Transmission: | 5-speed manual |

**Performance:**

| | |
|---|---:|
| Top speed, mph | 198 (217 with long gearing) |
| 0-60 mph, seconds | 3.5 |
| Quarter-mile, seconds | NA |

| | |
|---|---:|
| **Approximate price:** | $393,000 |

# FORD NASCAR THUNDERBIRD

**W**inston Cup drivers thunder around a 2.5-mile, high-banked superspeedway in less than 45 seconds, battling for position with 30 to 40 other cars. They race *inches* apart at speeds where air turbulence can buffet one of these 3,000-pound machines a yard sideways without warning. There *is* no margin for error.

They torture their engines, running at a constant 6000 rpm and wringing from the production-based powerplants more than 625 horsepower. The motors gulp half a gallon of fuel during each 2.5-mile lap while steeply banked corners subject the drivers to lateral forces as great as 2.2 gs.

This is the world of Bill Elliott. One of NASCAR's most competitive drivers, "Awesome Bill from Dawnsonville" and his Ford Thunderbird are synonymous with record-setting Winston Cup action.

Elliott in 1985 set an international 500-mile closed course race-speed record by averaging 186.288 mph while winning the Winston 500 at Alabama International Motor Speedway. And just when everyone thought that stock car speeds could go no higher, he and his fire-breathing T-Bird charged to a new, all-time NASCAR qualifying speed of 212.809 mph at Talledega in 1987.

In 1988, Elliott notched five superspeedway wins and became the first Ford driver to win a NASCAR season championship since 1969, when David Pearson did it in a Holman-Moody-prepared Torino.

Elliott got a new car for '89, still a Thunderbird, but one of a slightly different—and smoother—feather. Ford's all-new '89 T-Bird, the most aerodynamic Thunderbird ever, hit the showrooms in December

1988 and the racetracks in February 1989. You could hear the cheers at Ford's Special Vehicle Operations, the company's racing arm. The new T-Bird looks as if it were made for racing, with a silhouette that minimizes airflow separation for less turbulence and minimal drag.

Though its prow is less pointed than before, the new T-Bird's nose combines with a flatter hood and higher rear decklid to improve the car's downforce and aerodynamic balance. With flush-mounted window glass, four degrees more rake to the windshield, and a steeper slope to the rear window, it boasts one of the sleekest shapes on the road. No minor detail escapes detection —even the taillights are softened in angle, lending to the overall drag coefficient of 0.32 on the production model and laying the groundwork for a truly slippery racing car.

Under the street-version's hood is a 3.8-liter 90-degree V-6. Taking a cue from drag racing, the new Thunderbird Super Coupe uses the first modern-day production engine with a positive-displacement Roots-type supercharger. Intercooled and with dual exhausts, the SC's supercharged 3.8 is good for 210 horsepower and 315 pounds/feet of torque.

For Winston Cup competition, the V-6 is supplanted by a cast-iron, 358-cubic-inch small-block V-8 bored out from the standard Ford SVO 351-cubic-inch engine. The racing engine has a bore of 3.5 inches with 0.030 over, and it carries an average stroke of 3.5 inches from bottom to top dead center. Cubic centimeters of volume and compression ratios on the powerplant vary from track to track. The

Ford's streamlined 1989 Thunderbird (**opposite page**) took to the NASCAR wars like a champion. It's capable of a 205-mph top speed. Silhouette must conform to production car's (**top**), though stock wheelbase has to be shortened three inches for racing, and fenders are slightly flared (**above**). Engine is a 358-cubic-inch V-8 (**left**). Its high-performance cast-aluminum heads, block, and internal components are over-the-counter parts. It has 640 horsepower without carburetor restriction plates, and about 390 with them.

Daytona, the two fastest tracks. The plates slice horsepower from about 640 to roughly 390. Elliott and other competitors have countered with new methods of utilizing compression, and fuel and air pressure. In the intake manifold area, there are new plenum shapes, sizes and running configurations, and attention also is being paid to the exhaust chambers.

But all this technology is useless without the skill and guile to put it to use. Take Elliott's suspension setup at the Michigan International Speedway in June 1989. During the early laps, his new Thunderbird was programmed with a slight "push" all the way through the corners. Shrewd adjustments during pit stops—altering wedge, weight and stagger—brought its handling to a more neutral state that met the changing demands of the track. He rocketed to victory.

The Michigan experience is important, because an earlier crash involving Elliott and his new car had delayed extensive on-track testing. It's the kind of canny move displayed in Michigan that has put Awesome Bill among the NASCAR greats. And in the 180-mph knife fight that is Winston Cup racing, he's confident Ford's fresh new Thunderbird has the right stuff to keep him there.

Dashboard of NASCAR Thunderbird (**opposite page, top left**) is all business. Bill Elliott, 1988 Winston Cup champion, at the office (**opposite page, top right**). The NASCAR T-Bird's thin sheet-metal body attaches to a pure-racing chassis that incorporates a sturdy roll cage and a fire-suppression system to protect the driver. Quick pit work by Elliott's professional crew (**opposite page, bottom**) is a key to his winning ways. Trunk-lid spoiler can be adjusted for size and angle to tailor aerodynamics to a particular track (**left**).

high-performance cast-aluminum heads, block, and internal components are over-the-counter parts, listed in Ford's SVO catalog.

The NASCAR Thunderbird's sheet-metal body attaches to the racing chassis using modified roll bars and mounting bars. The car's wheelbase is shortened from production specs of 113 inches to racing's mandated 110. NASCAR requires that its body shape and dimensions match those of the street version, the only change being a slight flaring of the racing machine's fender wells to accommodate the fat Goodyear tires.

Adhering to the dictum of different horses for different courses, Elliott's Thunderbirds can be mechanically altered to meet the challenge of a particular racecourse. For example, on 27 of the 29 Winston Cup tracks, Elliott locates the car's tie rods and center links forward of the front spindle. This helps keep the rear end planted to the track in turns. For the 24-degree banked oval at Atlanta and the one-mile oval at Richmond, the hardware is mounted aft of the spindle, which encourages the car's tail to swing wide in the turns, behavior Elliott prefers on those courses.

To negotiate the two tight road courses, Watkins Glen and Sears Point, a 4-speed Jerico transmission handles the required 10 to 14 shifts per lap. This rugged gear box uses no clutch and a skilled driver like Elliott can coax the shift lever through its H-shaped gate very quickly indeed.

While the basic stock-car chassis has remained largely unaltered for more than a decade, the new frontier of aerodynamics has taken NASCAR technology from under the shade tree and into the wind tunnel. From their conception, race cars are now tested to improve air flow over, under, and around their bodies. With NASCAR striving for parity in horsepower, aerodynamics has become a vital battleground in the hunt for the few seconds per lap that spell the difference between winners and also-rans. At the same time, new tire compounds are being developed for a better grip of the racing surface.

Elliott's high-speed records signaled a kind of flashpoint for NASCAR. Officials had already clamped a limit on cubic-inch displacement, but the racers' skill at fine tuning, especially their intake-manifold wizardry, soon produced horsepower once reserved only for the big-blocks. Not long after Elliott's record-braking runs, NASCAR instituted carburetor restriction plates at Talledega and

## 1989 Ford Thunderbird NASCAR Coupe Major Specifications

**Manufacturer:**

Melling Racing, Dawsonville, Ga./Banjo's Performance Center, Arden, N.C./ Melling Racing Team

**Dimensions:**

| | |
|---|---|
| Wheelbase, in. | 110.0 |
| Overall length, in. | 198.7 |
| Overall width, in. | 71.1 |
| Overall height;, in. | 50.5 |
| Track (front), in. | 60.5 |
| Track (rear), in. | 60.5 |
| Curb weight, lbs. | 3500 |

**Powertrain:**

| | |
|---|---|
| Layout: | front-engine, rear-wheel drive |
| Engine type: | overhead-valve V-8 (aluminum heads) |
| Displacement, liters/cubic inches | NA/385 |
| Horsepower @ rpm | 625 @ NA |
| Torque (lbs./ft.) @ rpm | 500 @ NA |
| Fuel delivery: | 4-barrel carburetor |
| Transmission: | (oval tracks) 4-speed manual (road courses) Jerico 4-speed |

**Performance:**

| | |
|---|---|
| Top speed, mph | 205 |
| 0-60 mph, seconds | NA |
| Quarter-mile, seconds | NA |

| | |
|---|---|
| **Approximate price:** | $85,000 |

# BOB GLIDDEN
# FORD PROBE

From beneath the quivering bodywork comes the mad rumba beat of a monster V-8. Coasting to the starting line, Bob Glidden suddenly gooses the throttle and a roaring cannonade of noise rolls across the staging apron at the 1988 National Hot Rod Association Supernationals. His car settles, then inches toward the starting beam. Within seconds it will be rifling down the quarter-mile strip, Glidden's helmet pinned to the headrest, his fire-proof-gloved right hand snatching four quick shifts while his left steers with a hundred minute course corrections.

The moments before the start of a drag race are always heart-pounding, though Glidden has been here many times before. In fact, no drag racer has won more NHRA national events than Bob Glidden. But today is different. Glidden and his family team are running a new car. Their Motorcraft Ford Probe has a lot to prove in this hotly contested world of Pro Stock, a 180-mph world where the difference between the fastest and slowest runner in a 16-car field is less than two-tenths of a second; a world in which cars rush past 60 mph from a standing start even before their clutch is fully out; a world where victory margins are commonly measured in hundredths of a second. Not only is this Glidden's very first race with the Probe, it's also his first since retiring his record-setting Ford Thunderbird. With that car he won an unprecedented eight national drag events in 1987, including one in which he set the NHRA Pro Stock speed record of 191.32 mph on his way to a third consecutive NHRA Pro-Stock World Championship.

So while Glidden's red-white-and-blue Probe has lot to prove as it sits on the starting line here at the Supernationals in Baytown, Texas, it also has two formidable weapons. The first is Glidden himself. A native of the central-Indiana town of Whiteland (population, 2000), Glidden entered the Pro Stock wars in 1973 and captured back-to-back Winston Pro Stock national titles in '74 and '75. Glidden won the title in '78, '79, and '80, then tore off another three wins, '85–'87. He dominates the field, winning 80 percent of his elimination rounds—the best record of any professional drag racer. Glidden is the first to credit his team for his success. His wife, Etta, is crew chief of a family effort that also includes sons Bill and Rusty, who, along with their dad, do most of the engine work.

Weapon No. 2 would be the Probe. From the outside, it looks like

Smokey burnouts help heat the Motorcraft Probe's rear tires to provide better traction off the line (**opposite page**). Unassuming-looking Bob Glidden (**below**) possesses the talent needed to harness 1100 horsepower as his Pro-Stock Probe explodes away from the starting gate on another sub-eight-second sprint. No professional drag racer has a better winning percentage than Glidden.

Pro-Stock Probe retains the production car's silhouette, but uses a full-race 497-cubic inch V-8 (**opposite page, top left**) and a cabin fortified for the rigors of competition (**opposite page, right**). Glidden broke his own NHRA elapsed time record on the Probe's very first run, then went on to win the 1988 Pro Stock world's championship, his unprecedented ninth national title.

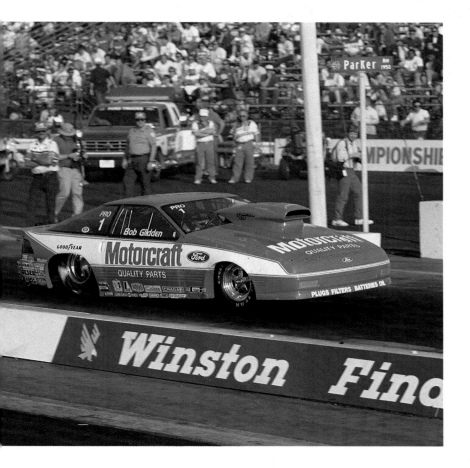

## Bob Glidden Ford Probe Major Specifications

**Manufacturer:**

Jerry Haas Race Cars, St. Louis, Missouri/Glidden Family Racing, Whiteland, Indiana

**Dimensions:**

| | |
|---|---|
| Wheelbase, in. | 101.0 |
| Overall length, in. | 179.0 |
| Overall width, in. | 69.0 |
| Overall height;, in. | 46.0 |
| Track (front), in. | 55.0 |
| Track (rear), in. | 43.0 |
| Curb weight, lbs. | 2350 |

**Powertrain:**

| | |
|---|---|
| Layout: | front-engine, rear-wheel drive |
| Engine type: | V-8 |
| Displacement, liters/cubic inches | NA/497 |
| Horsepower @ rpm | est. 1100 @ 8200 |
| Torque (lbs./ft.) @ rpm | 770 @ 6800 |
| Fuel delivery: | two 4-barrel Holley carburetors |
| Transmission: | Lenco 4-speed manual |

**Performance:**

| | |
|---|---|
| Top speed, mph | 189.91 |
| 0-60 mph, seconds | NA |
| Quarter-mile, seconds | 7.277 |

| | |
|---|---|
| **Approximate price:** | $110,000-$120,000 |

any other street-going Ford subcompact coupe. Well, OK, maybe a highly altered subcompact coupe, one with a lowered stance and a hood scoop that could be headgear for the queen creature in *Aliens*. But it's clearly a Probe. Drag racing's rulesmakers strive to maintain strong visual links to the production cars upon which Pro Stockers are based. That's why Glidden's Probe must use a wheelbase that's within one percent of a production model's. It has to retain the factory sheetmetal roof and rear quarter panels, and its doors must open on hinges. Its windshield must be the factory glass; the windows can be plastic, but they must keep the production shape. The rest of the body can be of composite plastics or aluminum, but must conform to the production Probe's silhouette.

To prevent Glidden from radically altering the car's basic weight distribution, the rules say the Probe's front-wheel axis must line up with the engine's forward-most spark plug. His driver's seat and steering wheel have to be in the factory position. And the interior must have room for two seats. But any further similarity to factory Probes ends here.

Long gone are drag racing's Super Stock cars, those 1960s crowd pleasers that actually were production-line models, if highly modified and factory-massaged ones. Pro Stock replaced Super Stock in 1969 and is its descendent in spirit only.

Beneath the skin of Glidden's car is a full-race tubular frame chassis/roll cage fitted with a custom-built suspension. Nothing down here is available over the counter. Factory equipment consists of little more than spark plugs, filters, and lubricants. Where the rear cargo area of the factory Probe would be, Glidden's car houses dual batteries for the electric starting system and a bladder fuel cell. In front, where the stock Probe's transversely mounted 4- or 6-cylinder engines drive the front wheels, Glidden's car packs an all-aluminum V-8 that powers the rear wheels. Based on Ford's famed Boss 429 NASCAR engine of the late '60s, Glidden's V-8 displaces 497 cubic inches. It drives through a Lenco 4-speed transmission, a Pro-Stock staple that Glidden shifts by snatching four separate gear levers that sprout like branches from the tunnel next to his thin plastic shell of a seat.

No form of motorsports is purer or more American than drag racing. Two cars line up side by side and from a standing start race one another over a quarter mile. First one across the finish line wins. Period. Of course, nothing is so simple as it seems. Modern-day drag racing actually consists of multiple categories of weight and power classes overlaid with a bewildering handicapping system that enables cars of vastly different performance to compete against one another. Only in the professional categories do the cars run "heads up," that is, without handicaps. This is where Glidden competes, and wins.

He guards his secrets closely. Like all Pro Stockers, Glidden must leave the line quickly and cleanly, underway within a fraction of second once the green "go" light flashes. He must get just the right trace of wheel spin from the 16-inch-wide racing slicks, while not letting the 4.5-inch-wide front tires stray too far or lift too high. Beyond Glidden's obvious driving skill, his success lies in the way his family team prepares his engines, and in the way in which it arranges the car's weight distribution.

All this comes into play as Glidden launches the Probe on its maiden voyage. The nose rises, the slicks hook up, the tail gives a slight wiggle as Glidden corrects his course. The Probe is composed now, gaining speed. Its snout hugs the pavement as the Ford howls toward the finish-line timing beam. It rips through in 7.277 seconds. In his first race in the car, Glidden has set a new NHRA Pro-Stock elapsed-time record. The old NHRA mark of 7.318 seconds, by the way, was his, too. Glidden's speed in the Probe's first race is 189.91. (Running under International Hot Rod Association rules, which allow engine displacements of around 700 cubic inches compared to the NHRA's maximum 500, Glidden's Thunderbird in 1987 set the all-time Pro Stock speed record, 199.11 mph. A similar Motorcraft T-Bird driven by Rickie Smith in '87 set the IHRA E.T. mark of 7.172 seconds.)

Glidden's elation at the Probe's record-shattering inaugural run is short lived, however. The team can't seem to unlock the new car's speed on a consistent basis. They can't even get past the second elimination round until the sixth race of the season. But then the Probe begins to perform. Glidden is once again shutting down opponents cold. The Probe becomes as feared as his Thunderbird was. By season's end, the Motorcraft Ford Probe has won seven Pro Stock events, bringing Glidden's career total to 67, 30 more than the next closest competitor. It also has captured for drag racer extraordinaire Bob Glidden his ninth NHRA Pro Stock National Championship.

# FORD RS 200

Authorities dissolved the wild Group B category, Europe's controversial competition for production-based rally cars, before Ford's RS 200 (**both pages**) could make its mark. But Ford went ahead and built the 200 models it had promised and they brought to the street such racing features as a durable multi-shock suspension (**left**) and light-weight body/frame construction (**right and above**).

When Ford-UK decided to develop a new competition car for the mid-1980s, it made no compromises. Like the new car's rivals—machines like the Peugeot 205 Turbo 16 and the Lancia Delta S4—Ford's 2- and 4-wheel-drive thunderbolt is designed to win high-speed rallies, not to please its boulevard-cruising customers.

Those customers who never edged a tire onto a race course could still plan to drive an RS 200 into the home garage, though. Stuart Turner, Ford's motorsports director, told *Road & Track* that "We expect to sell them to the public. The break-even point will be the initial batch of 200, but we plan to build a lot more." Reality intervened, however, and the total number produced fell short of Turner's lofty prediction.

According to the regulations Ford had to meet, only 200 cars had to be built to qualify for the International Group B category. That's exactly how many were produced by Ford. In fact, the car's name—RS 200—stands for "Rallye Sport, 200 built," a very succinct reminder of the car's purpose (and rarity). It was a single-purpose machine, whose function had to take precedence over refinement.

The project was conceived in 1983, and the first car rolled out the next year. All 200 cars were hastily assembled in a redundant Reliant factory in the British Midlands during the winter of 1985-86. Some of them are finished in stripped-out rally trim, with sliding windows and no carpeting. Others are completely equipped for road use with conventional wind-down windows, interior lighting, a clock, and some stowage room. Although the cockpit is quite noisy, some owners have fitted their RS 200s with radios and even cellular telephones. Quite a lot of the cockpit "furniture" is lifted from other current Ford cars, such as the Sierra and the European-style Escort. Some have right-hand steering, while others are left-hand drive. All of them were originally painted white with dark grey interiors, so individual sponsors' color schemes could easily be added by the customers.

Chassis layout is more like that of a race car than anything meant to be driven on the road. The massively strong platform-type chassis structure has some steel members, but also makes use of highly advanced composite material, including carbon fiber and on the fully tuned competition cars, Kevlar.

The engine is mounted behind the 2-seater cabin, with the main transmission between the passenger footwells. The coupe design came from Filippo Sapino at Ford's Ghia subsidiary in Italy and is made out of fiberglass body skins. After a great deal of development effort in the wind tunnel and out on the track, the body picked up upward-facing radiator outlets in the nose and a large wrap-around aerodynamic spoiler that develops downforce as the car's speed increases.

The only Ford production-based mechanical unit in the RS 200 is the engine, which is known as the BTD. This is a turbocharged version of the famous Ford-Cosworth BDA engine, a light-alloy 4-cylinder 16-valve dual-overhead-cam design previously used in the Escort RS1600 and RS1800. In the standard RS 200 the engine is 110-cubic inches (1.8-liters), though in special "Evolution" cars—later built for motorsport events—the engine displaces 130 cubic inches (2.1 liters).

Because there is plenty of space in the engine bay area, the Garrett T03/T04 turbocharger is mounted well clear of the engine on the right side. Ducting leads boost air to an air-to-air intercooler, which is mounted under a scoop behind the roof panel. Cooled air is then directed to the Bosch-fuel-injected intake manifold on the car's left side.

In standard form the engine produces 250 horsepower—an impressive 139 horsepower per liter—though it's capable of much more. When cars were delivered, customers could order 300-horsepower, 350-horsepower, or even "full-house" 450-horsepower engine tunes.

Drive from the engine goes forward to a 5-speed main gearbox. The transmission is capable of providing "free 4-wheel-drive+" (controled by no fewer than three viscous coupling limited-slip differentials), "locked 4-wheel-drive" (where the center differential is locked up for use in extremely slippery conditions), or rear-drive only. A second "mode-change" lever that controls these choices is normally omitted from the road cars, which instead run in "free" 4-wheel-drive all the time.

*Its acceleration matches that of the Ferrari 308 GTB, but the top speed of Ford's 4-cylinder supercar is held to about 145 mph by a body design that induces aerodynamic downforce.*

Bred for the demands of big-league European rallying, the 4-wheel-drive RS 200 can travel swiftly on wet and slippery surfaces (**below and bottom**). The car has found a home, however, in the driveways of wealthy enthusiasts (**right**), who appreciate its rarity—only 148 were actually delivered—and its place at motoring's cutting edge. Its twin-cam, turbo four pours out up to 250 horsepower per liter, its suspension and all-wheel drive conquer any road, and its body, fashioned of space-age materials, is aesthetically arresting.

The RS 200 is no longer than a U.S.-style Escort, but wider and heavier—a pure sports car with little storage capacity but with magnificent grip, handling, and "balance," all combined with a surprisingly supple ride.

Standard top speed is in the vicinity of 145 mph; acceleration matches the pace of cars like the Ferrari 308 GTB. Top speed is limited by the body downforce—a slippery shape, not intended to maximize tire grip, could certainly have helped push the maximum up to 160 mph. The RS 200 is at its best once the engine is singing along at more than 4000 rpm, and truly hits its stride on fast and sweeping roads. Interstate travel can grow boring, since the car simply isn't being extended to its peak at legal speeds.

Although not an ideal car for use in heavy traffic (for one thing, rearward visibility is restricted), the RS 200 is flexible and reliable enough for that purpose. Not for nothing did Ford-UK cover it with the same warranty applied to all its mass-production family cars.

The Group B category in rallying was canceled in 1986, before many RS 200s had been delivered to private customers. For a while, it looked as if the survivors would simply be scrapped. But Ford continued to develop the machine, especially for road use. More than 50 of the cars in stock were stripped out to provide a bigger parts stock, and a total of 148 were eventually delivered, the last in the early months of 1989.

These cars were often prepared to special order. Some have a new body color, some carry special seats and trim, and one or two flaunt full air conditioning. Certain examples were striped to replicate the "works" competition cars. Unfortunately, most went into static collections and may not be seen again until the inevitable rise in value, which always seems to follow limited editions as they age a bit.

When sales began at the end of 1986, an RS 200 could be had for about $82,000. By 1989, when customers were paying for all manner of extras, a typical invoice price approached $108,000. A few cars were sold in the U.S. and Canada. The RS 200's price, in almost *every* country in the world, was higher than the cost of most Porsches and Ferraris. Even so, Ford had little difficulty in selling every one of the cars it made.

## Ford RS 200 Major Specifications

**Manufacturer:**
Ford Motor Co. Ltd. (Ford of Europe); Brentwood, England
Assembly by Reliant Motor Co.

**Dimensions:**

| | |
|---|---|
| Wheelbase, in. | 99.6 |
| Overall length, in. | 157.5 |
| Overall width, in. | 69.0 |
| Overall height, in. | 52.0 |
| Track (front), in. | 59.1 |
| Track (rear), in. | 59.0 |
| Curb weight, lbs. | 2602 |

**Powertrain:**

| | |
|---|---|
| Layout: | mid-engine, rear-wheel or four-wheel drive |
| Engine type: | turbocharged, intercooled double-overhead-cam 4-cylinder |
| Displacement, liters/cubic inches | 1.8/110 |
| Horsepower @ rpm | 250 @ 6500 (300/350/450 available) |
| Torque (lbs./ft.) @ rpm | 215 @ 45000 |
| Fuel delivery: | Electronic fuel injection |
| Transmission: | 5-speed manual |

**Performance:**

| | |
|---|---|
| Top speed, mph | 147.0 |
| 0-60 mph, seconds | 5.1; 2.6 (Evolution) |
| Quarter-mile, seconds | 12.3;10.2 (Evolution) |

| | |
|---|---|
| **Approximate price:** | $63,000 (initial) |

# SALEEN MUSTANG SSC

For Steve Saleen, turning a Mustang into a race winner has become an art form. His years of racing and Sports Car Club of America Endurance Series Championship competition suggest that there isn't much he can't do with Ford's ponycar. Saleen's efforts peak with the SSC, which stands for "Saleen Super Car." And a super performer it is, able to run right up to 150 miles an hour while differing just enough in appearance from a stock Mustang GT to attract envious stares from knowledgeable passersby.

Saleen starts with the Mustang LX 5.0L Sport, which repeatedly has garnered "best-performance-buy-for-the-buck" honors from auto critics. The cars arrive at his Anaheim, California, shop as low-budget muscle cars, and roll out as total-performance Mustangs, with all the refinement and quality, power and handling of a high-buck EuroRocket. Yet, they remain truly all-American. The SSC is a tribute to Mustang's quarter-century birthday, and Saleen Autosports has set a clear-cut goal: to make the SSC one of the world's premiere driving machines.

The Saleen shop applies its knowledge and ability to the interior, exterior, and driveline to produce a thoroughly re-engineered Mustang. The end result is Steve Saleen's vision of the perfect ponycar.

The heart of the SSC is a new high-specification engine that comes close to one horsepower per cubic inch in fully streetable trim. The already-potent 302-cubic-inch, 225-horsepower mill, standard Ford issue, gets ported heads and larger 1.90-inch diameter intake valves.

The intake manifold is also ported to match the heads. A more potent roller-rocker camshaft from Ford's Special Vehicle Operations is part of the package, along with SVO 1.7:1-ratio rocker arms. A larger 65-mm throttle body replaces the stock 60-mm unit. Ford's electronic fuel injection gets a recalibrated MAFS (Mass Air Flow Sensor), while the electronic engine management computer is also recalibrated. All SSC Mustangs bear a "premium fuel only" sticker for best performance, even though the stock compression ratio of 9:1 is retained. Scavenger-type Walker Dynomax stainless steel tubular headers are included. All of this effort results in a fully emissions-certified engine by Ford.

Under the hood, a triangular body brace is installed between the upper shock towers and the cowl. It frames the car's special cast aluminum intake, which bears the designation "SALEEN SSC."

*Aftermarket modifier and race-car driver Steve Saleen starts with a stock 5-liter Mustang LX and turns it into the Saleen Super Car (**both pages**). Modifications to Ford's V-8 bump horsepower from a stock 225 to a hot 292, while competition-bred suspension alterations and wider tires whip the pony car into a pony express. Unlike the 2+2 factory Mustang, the SSC is strictly a 2-seater.*

To handle an increase of around 65 horsepower, to at least 290, a heavy-duty clutch and pressure plate couple the power to a special SVO T5 5-speed transmission fitted with new ratio gears. A higher-specification 3.55:1 posi-traction rear axle assembly also is installed.

Gorgeous 5-spoke 16 × 8-inch high-strength cast aluminum wheels by DP Sport Wheels get P225/50ZR16 General XP tires up front and P245/50ZR16 tires on the rear. Stopping power gets a boost from SVO grooved brake rotors with heavy-duty caliper components.

Monroe electronically controlled Formula GP three-way struts and shock absorbers improve the handling to match the car's brute performance. A console switch allows driver selection of ride quality. Front and rear anti-sway bars (1.31-inch diameter in front, .89-inch at the rear) hold down the car through tight turns.

Skid pad estimates show the SSC to be in the .88g range or higher. The rival Ferrari Testarossa rates .87g, but at four times the cost of a $36,500 SSC. Want to out-handle a Lamborghini Countach that costs six times as much as this special-edition Saleen Mustang? The SSC can manage that while beating the 0-60 mph and quarter-mile times *and* skid pad potential of a $41,000 Porsche 944S.

One of the best and most beautiful Mustangs yet conceived has a handsome graphics package that combines the best of SVO, Ford, and Saleen. It includes a race-developed front air dam, side skirts, rear valence, and a whale-tail spoiler. Special contour seats with lumbar supports are part of the interior. There's a premium sound system and subtle improvements for enhanced driver comfort include air conditioning and cruise control. A Momo leather-wrapped steering wheel sits at a slightly different angle than usual.

As your glance drops to the 200-mph speedometer, you're reminded that this is a serious machine. Serious to the tune of 0-60 in 6 seconds flat and 150-mph top. Considering the relatively modest SSC price tag, that's serious enough to tempt many a supercar fan who lacks a limitless cash flow.

The SSC saddles up for the open road with Saleen-developed aerodynamic bodywork and a taut suspension that keep its nose down and tail straight, no matter what the speed (**left**). Given free rein, the SSC will gallop to more than 145 mph. A "Saleen" windshield decal and distinctive gold and gray bodyside graphics brand this Mustang as a thoroughbred not to be trifled with.

Clockwise, from above: the SSC gets SVO grooved brake rotors with heavy-duty calipers and Monroe electronically controlled Formula GP three-way struts and shocks; stock rear seat gives way to a high-powered stereo speaker system; 16 × 8-inch high-strength cast aluminum wheels by DP Sport wear 50-series rubber; a triangular body brace frames the car's special cast aluminum intake manifold; the SSC boasts a throaty exhaust note, razor-sharp steering, and racer-like road manners.

## Saleen Mustang SSC Major Specifications

**Manufacturer:**

Saleen Autosport; Anaheim, California

**Dimensions:**

| | |
|---|---|
| Wheelbase, in. | 100.5 |
| Overall length, in. | 179.6 |
| Overall width, in. | 69.1 |
| Overall height, in. | 50.0 |
| Track (front), in. | 57.3 |
| Track (rear), in. | 57.8 |
| Curb weight, lbs. | 3450 |

**Powertrain:**

| | |
|---|---|
| Layout: | front-engine, rear-wheel drive |
| Engine type: | overhead-valve V-8 |
| Displacement, liters/cubic inches | 4.9/302 |
| Horsepower @ rpm | 292 @ 5200 |
| Torque (lbs./ft.) @ rpm | 327 @ 3500 |
| Fuel delivery: | port fuel injection |
| Transmission: | 5-speed manual |

**Performance:**

| | |
|---|---|
| Top speed, mph | est. 149 |
| 0-60 mph, seconds | est. 5.9 |
| Quarter-mile, seconds | est. 14.2 |

| **Approximate price:** | $20,000 |
|---|---|

# JAGUAR XJ-S

**T**raditional elegance. That's one way to describe the most potent production car from Britain's Jaguar—a company well acquainted with tradition, in both the best and worst senses of the word. Even more than its rakish and rapid XK ancestors, the latest top-of-the-line coupe and convertible mix a broad palette of creature comforts with some sizzling road performance.

Consider the combination of a silky V-12 engine, effortless power sent through a smooth 3-speed automatic transmission, air-conditioned

Jaguar introduced the XJ-S in 1975 as the successor to its timeless XK-E. A targa body style followed in '83, but it wasn't until the full convertible model (**below**) bowed in '88 that that classic cat had a worthy heir. A V-12 beneath its bonnet, the Jag drop top has 156 body panels that are distinct from the XJ-S coupe, including a more rakishly angled windshield.

comfort with the smell of real leather all around, sunlight glinting off polished walnut facia and door cappings. Sound irresistible? Ordinarily, yes—but not always when combined in the form of the Jaguar XJ-S, even though its many attributes include a top speed beyond 140 miles per hour.

Not many cars start their career with a good reputation, lose it progressively in the first few years, then get it all back before reaching their tenth anniversary. Jaguar's XJ-S model, so confidently introduced in 1975 and so despised by 1980, is a perfect example of just that sort of situation.

At the end of the 1970s everything was going wrong for Jaguar. The cars had unmistakable styling, splendid engines, great refinement, and (considering their size and weight) remarkable handling. On the debit side, they also tended to be unreliable and to suffer from premature corrosion. And potential customers knew it.

Then, with the company at crisis point, John Egan arrived to take over the helm. With a great deal of effort (and not a little self-satisfied trumpeting from corporate publicists), the downhill slide was reversed. The XJ-S, whose sales had shrunk to less than 2,000 a year, doubled, then redoubled by the late 1980s. All this gain was helped along by the introduction of the more powerful and fuel-efficient "HE" (High Efficiency) engine.

If customers were unhappy with the XJ-S as a whole in its middle years, they certainly didn't complain about its specifications. The underpan of the XJ-S of that period is a shortened version of the XJ6/XJ12 design, which had first gone on sale in 1968/1969. That means supple, long-travel independent suspension at front and rear, four-wheel disc brakes, power-assisted steering—plus an almost incredibly high standard of refinement, which seems to insulate passengers completely from the road and all that is happening around them.

Central to the design is a fuel-injected version of the 326-cubic inch (5.3-liter) alloy single-cam V-12 engine, which had first been used in the Series III XK-E of 1971. For XJ-S purposes it had been retouched and repackaged, able to produce around 300 horsepower without temperament, and apparently with little effort.

Compared with, say, a Ferrari V-12 engine, the Jaguar design is almost completely silent. You can stand alongside an idling Jag and never know the engine is ticking over. As in the V-12 Jaguar saloons of this period, the engine is matched to a 3-speed automatic transmission.

The styling of the XJ-S, on the other hand, could best be described as controversial. Although still a large and bulky car, originally offered only as a closed coupe with cramped 2+2 seating, it's also wide and flamboyant. Perhaps most important, it is by no means as

dignified as its Jaguar contemporaries. The problem is focused on the rear quarters, where panels rather like the flying buttresses of an old building crowd in on each side of a small rear window.

None of this matters in a healthy XJ-S, for the car is always fast enough to sweep every care away. Seemingly without effort it can zip rapidly up to 130 mph and beyond, and in ideal conditions may reach about 155 mph. Speeds beyond that level, with the car's rather large frontal area and the none-too-slippery shape of the bodywork, aren't possible.

Driving an XJ-S fast is a rather eerie business, though, for there's no apparent effort in the production of all the power needed to thrust the 4,000-pound car to high speeds. Unless the windows are rolled down, it all happens in most impressive silence. Compared with other, more costly supercars, driving the Jag *slowly* is easy, too. This engine seems as happy while lazily turning over at 1000 rpm as it is when reaching for 5000 rpm and beyond.

Once the XJ-S's future had been secured in the early 1980s, Jaguar finally began to develop it further. First, at the end of 1983, came the launch of the Cabriolet body style. Rather like the Porsche 911 Targa, it features a removable roof panel but a fixed rear window. For all practical purposes the car is a 2-seater, lacking the rear-compartment head and leg room needed to carry grown-up passengers in any

At around $60,000, 192 inches of overall length, and 4,200 pounds of curb weight, the XJ-S Convertible (**below, left**) is a real indulgence of a 2-seater. Still, its silken V-12, sexy looks, and British luxury-performance aura offset most any drawback. Its coupe counterpart (**below**) is one of the world's premier long-distance grand-touring cars, offering speed, silence, and a remarkably supple ride.

153

degree of comfort. At the same time, the car offers what was a brand-new 6-cylinder engine option: the twin-cam, 24-valve AJ6 design, also intended for use in the next-generation Jaguar sedan. Naturally this isn't as powerful as the V-12, but is strong enough to give the European-spec car a top speed of about 140 mph.

Two years after the Cabriolet's introduction, Jaguar mated the body style to the V-12 engine. Although this is a less aerodynamically efficient shape, the car's top speed remains about 145 mph.

Finally, in the spring of 1988—more than 12 years after the original XJ-S went into production—Jaguar launched a convertible version. This is the very first XJ-S to have a completely fold-away soft top. (It's power-operated, of course, and can be retracted in about 12 seconds.) But by no means is the convertible a simple extension of the Cabriolet theme. The windshield is located at a different angle and the assembly contains 156 different body panels. Many enthusiasts have unwisely gushed that the spirit of the much smaller, smoother-styled XK-E had been rekindled.

The XJ-S Convertible, measuring 15 ft. 8 in. long and weighing 4,050 pounds, is a real indulgence of a 2-seater. Still, at the 1989 U.S. price of $56,000, it runs thousands of dollars less than equivalent performance cars from Porsche. Thus revived, the XJ-S appears set to go on selling strongly into the 1990s.

*Rear of XJ-S coupe (**opposite page, top**) suffers from flying-buttress backlight. Below this nest of tubing is the famous 5.3-liter V-12 (**opposite page, left**). XJ-S has luxurious, if cramped, 2+2 seating (**opposite page, right**). Aftermarket firm Koenig equips XJ-S with a 5-speed manual gearbox, uprated suspension, and aero body aids (**above**).*

## Jaguar XJ-S Major Specifications

**Manufacturer:**

Jaguar plc; Coventry, England

**Dimensions:**

| | |
|---|---:|
| Wheelbase, in. | 102.0 |
| Overall length, in. | 191.7 |
| Overall width, in. | 70.6 |
| Overall height, in. | 47.8 |
| Track (front), in. | 58.6 |
| Track (rear), in. | 59.2 |
| Curb weight, lbs. | 4015 (convertible 4190) |

**Powertrain:**

| | |
|---|---:|
| Layout: | front-engine, rear-wheel drive |
| Engine type: | single overhead-cam V-12 |
| Displacement, liters/cubic inches | 5.3/326 |
| Horsepower @ rpm | 262 @ 5000 |
| Torque (lbs./ft.) @ rpm | 290 @ 3000 |
| Fuel delivery: | Lucas digital fuel injection |
| Transmission: | 3-speed automatic |

**Performance:**

| | |
|---|---:|
| Top speed, mph | 141 |
| 0-60 mph, seconds | est. 8.1 |
| Quarter-mile, seconds | est. 16.2 |

| | |
|---|---:|
| **Approximate price:** | $48,000 (convertible $57,000) |

# SILK CUT XJR-9 JAGUAR

Privately owned Jaguars returned the marque to the 24 Hours of LeMans in 1984 and again in '85, when one won its class. Its proud racing heritage thus rekindled, Jaguar itself launched a factory racing team. LeMans in '86 saw three XJR-6s run well (**opposite page**), but not finish. That effort paved the way for the XJR-9 (**below**), which, in 1988, became the first Coventry cat since 1957 to outright win the historic LeMans enduro.

Strange as it may seem, cigarette smokers are partly responsible for Jaguar's surge of auto-racing victories: Without the sponsorship of Britain's Silk Cut cigarettes, the XJR series might not have developed as it has, culminating in the recent XJR-9 with its 700-plus horsepower V-12 that can pull the car from 0-60 in just 3.3 seconds. Top speed is a blinding 230 mph. Needless to say, you won't see the XJR-9 idling next to you at a stoplight.

After a 20-year absence from the racing schedules, Jaguar returned to competition at Le Mans when Bob Tullius entered his Group 44 team in the great French classic in 1984. Two XJR-5 cars were raced, each running normally aspirated 6-liter (366 cubic-inch) V-12s that evolved from Jaguar's production engine. The Tullius Jags were IMSA cars designed for America's sports prototype series. One was leading the IMSA class at Le Mans, lying 5th overall in the hands of Brian Redman, Doc Bundy, and Tullius, when it was stopped by gearbox failure in the 22nd hour.

The Tullius team returned in '85, again with Jaguar's U.S.-company support but still privately owned, and again entered two cars. The lead car, driven by Tullius, Chip Robinson, and France's Claude Ballot-Lena, soldiered through the twice-around-the clock enduro (in the final hours hitting on just 11 cylinders), and won the IMSA category, finishing 13th overall. Car number two again experienced transmission problems.

The Group 44 performance at Le Mans created such a tremendous media blitz about Jaguar's successful return to racing that the factory laid down plans for an official team. Jaguar determined that racing offered far more exposure for its advertising money than any other means of reaching the public. So they contracted with the British firm of Tom Walkinshaw Racing (TWR) to design, build, and campaign new cars in the entire Sports Prototype World Championship series. This was a bold undertaking, but one that proved to be highly successful.

Representing the Jaguar factory, TWR returned the marque to competition by racing FIA Group C formula cars, and debuted at Mosport, Canada in August 1985. During the winter of 1985-86, media interest mushroomed and attracted the sponsorship of Gallaher International, the manufacturer of Silk Cut cigarettes. Now with additional corporate sponsorship, TWR was able to field one of the strongest teams ever seen in international race competition.

Under Silk Cut colors of purple, white, and gold, the prototype Jaguars roared onto the international motor racing scene at Silverstone in May 1986, when the team took its first victory. The 1000-kilometer event remains Great Britain's premier race, and the team of American Eddie Cheever and Britisher Derek Warwick wheeled their updated XJR-6 to Silk Cut's first triumph—and to huge public response. Thirty years had passed, but Jaguar was back.

Since this was a new team, the 1986 season was used primarily for development and learning. However, Jaguar fans worldwide cheered the entry of three Silk Cut XJR-6 cars at Le Mans '86. When the Warwick/Cheever/Louis Schlesser Jag ran as high 2nd position in the 17th hour, enthusiasm bordered on frenzy. But when a suspension member collapsed, the last of the cars was out of the running.

TWR applied what it had learned in 1986 to new cars, designated XJR-8, for the '87 season. Engines were updated to 7 liters (427 cubic inches, reminiscent of the 1967 Ford Mk IV Le Mans winner with that engine displacement). Many other refinements signaled an improved Jaguar threat to Porsche domination. That year, the TWR Jaguars dominated FIA Group C. They were almost unbeatable.

The XJR-8 was designed by Tony Southgate and built at Kidlington, Oxfordshire by Tom Walkinshaw Racing. This series of cars evolved from the previous XJR-6. Two types were built: "sprint" cars for the shorter, high-speed races and long-distance cars for Le Mans and

Jaguar campaigns under GTPrototype rules in the North American IMSA series, but LeMans is its premier event. That's why the dramatic 1988 LeMans victory of XJR-9 No. 2 (**right**) is so significant. Drivers Jan Lammers, Johnny Dumfries, and Andy Wallace held off the mighty Porsche 962C to win the 24-hour race by less than two minutes. Though the Mulsanne speed trap credited the XJR-9 with 240 mph, a skeptical Jaguar recognized only 229.

Silverstone (the XJR-8LM).

Throughout the '87 season, the Jags set new standards for world class competitors. The XJR-8 Jaguars won eight of ten rounds of the FIA schedule that year, and placed four drivers at the top of the international drivers' championship, led by Raul Boesel. Not only was Jaguar back, but both the company and its drivers were now champions—a pleasing development that had never occurred before.

Engine development was led by TWR's Allan Scott. The engine's position in the car was designed to be "recessed" forward, to reduce the overall length of the car and improve weight distribution. Although the Porsches had finally been vanquished (but remained always a threat), a new German rival appeared on the scene.

The Daimler-Benz factory team, headed by Switzerland's Peter Sauber, unveiled a new foe in the C9 Sauber Mercedes. These cars, running turbocharged 5-liter V-8 engines, always had more power than either the Jaguars or Porsches, but used more fuel—thus requiring more frequent fuel stops. In the first round of the '88 season at Jerez in Spain for the Cadiz 800 Km, the single Sauber Mercedes entry gave the 1987 World Champion TWR Jaguar team formidable opposition. The car won the pole position against three Jaguars and lasted, unexpectedly, through the race to win by 24.53 seconds over the latest Jaguar, the XJR-9 of Nielson/Watson/Wallace. The other two Jags retired with transmission shifter problems.

A few weeks later in the "battle royal" at Silverstone, a pair of Sauber Mercedes entries lined up against two XJR-9 Jags, defending British honor as the previous year's winner. Running two cars for the first time, the Sauber team displayed some problems but took the pole nevertheless, and promised to make a race of it. The ensuing wheel-to-wheel battle between the Silk Cut Jags and the AEG Olympia-sponsored Mercedes unfolded in a great race, but the XJR-9 Jaguar slowly showed its superiority when Martin Brundle and Eddie Cheever nudged out a half-minute victory. Brundle took the battle to the Mercedes cars during mid-race and fought for a six-second lead out of the pits, expanding that to more than ten seconds, all with a cracked rib that he'd sustained during testing. The remainder of the season, including victory at Le Mans in a stretch of four wins in a row, was a Jaguar-versus-Mercedes shootout. Porsche dropped to a distant third.

Although the XJR-8 and -9 Jaguars look similar, there are many subtle differences. Body shape using carbon fiber and lightweight composites is designed for downforce, but high-speed aerodynamics

is also a consideration. The XJR-8 generates about 70 percent more downforce than a Porsche 962C, and the XJR-9 improves upon that figure. Crew chief Roger Silman and chief engineer Tony Southgate (each car also has an engineer) continually search for more "advantages" over the competition.

Engine wizard Allan Scott is the man behind the 60-degree V-12. Beginning with aluminum block and head castings, the water-cooled engine carries a forged steel crankshaft running in seven main bearings. Valve actuation is by a single chain driving one cam per bank. In its latest form, each cam operates 4 valves per cylinder rather than the previous (and highly successful) 2-valve heads. Single spark plugs fire each chamber via an electronic management system. Bore and stroke of 94 × 84 mm is over-square, displacing 6995 cc. With a compression ratio of 12.8:1, the fleet cat turns out upwards of 750 horsepower at 7000 rpm, with 540 pounds/feet of torque peaking at 5500 rpm. Power is transferred by a March 5-speed transmission and hydraulically operated triple-plate clutch.

Chassis layout consists of a carbon fiber and Kevlar composite monocoque, with the engine and transmission being a stressed member carrying rear suspension loads. Suspension is conventional technology, but the carbon fiber brakes are definitely not. (They glow spectacularly red hot when used.) Wheels that measure 17 inches in diameter by 13-inches wide up front, and 19 × 15.25 on the rear, carry Dunlop Kevlar bias-ply tires exclusively (radials are said to be on the way). Total racing weight is around 1900 pounds.

Going against the reigning World Champion, competitors face the prototype Jaguar's performance of 0-60 mph in 3.3 seconds; 0-150 in just 11.1 seconds; and a standing start quarter-mile sprint time of 10.5 seconds, reaching 146 mph. A 184-mph standing-start kilometer is history after just 18.5 seconds. The cars are not the fastest when compared to turbocharged Porsche and Mercedes entries, but they have the advantage of no turbo lag. As a result, they exit turns more quickly and accelerate faster.

Buckled into the latest Jaguar, this is the sort of performance that allowed XJR-9 driver Martin Brundle to score 267 points during the 1988 season, leading Jean-Louis Schlesser's Sauber Mercedes tally of 259. The Silk Cut team took its second consecutive Sports Prototype World Championship, scoring 357 points to lead the second-place AEG Sauber Mercedes team by a huge margin of 79 points.

Jaguar's latest racing edition, the XJR-10, turns away from the formidable V-12 in favor of a 3.0-liter turbocharged V-6 engine.

The exigencies of aerodynamic design make for an ungainly looking, but effective, Jaguar tail (**opposite page, top**). XJR-9 runs a 7-liter V-12 in Europe and a 6-liter unit in the American IMSA series. Neither uses a turbocharger. The aluminum engine (**opposite page, bottom**) is set behind the 2-place cabin, and drives the rear wheels through a 5-speed manual racing transmission. The XJR-9 finished fourth at LeMans in '89, behind the winning Mercedes-Benz. Its XJR-10 successor turns away from the venerable V-12 in favor of a 3-liter turbocharged V-6.

## Silk Cut Jaguar XJR-9 Major Specifications

**Manufacturer:**

Jaguar plc; Coventry, England

**Dimensions:**

| | |
|---|---|
| Wheelbase, in. | est. 109.5 |
| Overall length, in. | 189.0 |
| Overall width, in. | 78.7 |
| Overall height, in. | 43.3 |
| Track (front), in. | est. 59.1 |
| Track (rear), in. | NA |
| Curb weight, lbs. | 1870 |

**Powertrain:**

| | |
|---|---|
| Layout: | mid-engine, rear-wheel drive |
| Engine type: | overhead-cam V-12 |
| Displacement, liters/cubic inches | 6.0/366 (U.S.) or 7.0/427 (Europe) |
| Horsepower @ rpm | 640-720 @ 7000 |
| Torque (lbs./ft.) @ rpm | 540 @ 5500 |
| Fuel delivery: | electronic fuel injection |
| Transmission: | 5-speed straight-cut manual |

**Performance:**

| | |
|---|---|
| Top Speed, mph | 230 |
| 0-60 mph, seconds | 3.3 |
| Quarter-mile, seconds | 10.5 |

| | |
|---|---|
| **Approximate price:** | over $500,000 |

# LAMBORGHINI COUNTACH

**M**ore than most supercars, today's Countach—including the 25th anniversary model of 1989—borders on the bizarre. Watching an eager enthusiast contort his way under the door, legs twisting to reach the floor, hips squirming to squeeze their way into the seat, might cause a less-informed observer to wonder just what the attraction of this spaceship-like vehicle might be. In addition to the car's unforgettable shape, the answer is simple: speed.

By the time Lamborghini unleashed the first Countach in 1971, the public had come to *expect* amazing new models from the Italian concern. Lamborghini had been selling cars only since 1964, but always aimed to match Ferrari—or better still, to surpass its famous competitor.

Like Ferrari, Lamborghini built extremely fast cars, in small quantities, selling them at extremely high prices to serious lovers of fast machinery. As with Ferrari, too, it helped if the customer had a well-developed sense of humor. That's because his high-priced exoticar was likely to suffer fits of temperament, to succumb to unreliability, and to demand the regular services of a highly skilled mechanic.

In the late 1960s, Lamborghini had startled the world with its Miura 2-seater, a 170-mph car with its V-12 engine transversely mounted behind the cabin. The Miura's replacement, called Countach, was even more advanced, even more striking, and equally as fast. The name *Countach*, incidentally, is an almost-polite expletive in the region where the cars were built—almost equivalent to "Jeez" in American English!

Although the early Countach looks superficially "normal" (for the period), it is quite extraordinary in detail. Inside, the twin seats are mounted well forward. The engine is fixed behind the cabin, driving the rear wheels.

Like the Miura before it, the Countach had been styled by Marcello Gandini at Bertone. Its shape was inspired by famous Bertone show cars, such as the Carabo. Apart from having rather sharp-edged lines and a very low, wide, flat snout, the car also sports "coleopter" doors. When opened, the doors fold upward and forward, instead of outward as in any conventional car. Although this makes it easier to exit from the car when parked in a confined space, the problems of extracting oneself from what appears to be an inverted cart are best not pondered too closely.

The hugely powerful four-cam V-12 engine, a 240-cubic-inch (3.9-liter) unit producing 375 horsepower in the first cars, is longitudinally mounted in the engine bay. However, it drives *forward* to the gearbox, which is between the seats. Transmission output goes by shaft through the sump of the engine, to a final-drive unit below and behind.

*Probably no automobile defines the term exotic car in the public mind better than Lamborghini's magnificent, outrageous, compelling Countach (**both pages**). Its name is an Italian expletive, while its design seems to be from another planet. The car debuted in 1971, but still looks fresh today.*

The first cars, dubbed LP400, were not delivered until 1974 (immediately after the first Energy Crisis had done its best to kill off all such potent machines). By the late 1980s, the design had been changed three times, with the engine enlarged and the exhaust system cleaned up. In addition, Lamborghini had achieved some success in making the car salable in the U.S.

Before the final model, called 5000 Quattrovalvole, went on sale in 1985, a total of 860 earlier Countach models had been built. The Quattrovalvole was so outstanding that Lamborghini found it could sell at least 150 cars a year, even at prices fast approaching $200,000.

The Quattrovalvole is the fastest and best-developed Countach of them all. It retains the 96.5-inch wheelbase and the all-coil-spring, fully-independent suspension of the original. The 2-seater coupe's lines are as wickedly attractive and unique as ever. Late-model Countach shells have extended wheelarches and a slightly modified front-end treatment. Quite a few are delivered with optional rear spoilers.

Since the early 1970s, the V-12 had been fighting a losing battle against exhaust emission laws. The Quattrovalvole features entirely new cylinder heads, still run by twin overhead camshafts, but now with 4 valves per cylinder. *Quattrovalvole*, logically enough, is the Italian way of saying "four valves."

Measuring 315 cubic inches (5.17 liters), the engine is colossally powerful. It produces a peak of 455 horsepower at 7000 rpm, positively singing up and down the range as the driver swaps gears. Except for the fact that it's wide (78.7 inches—the equal of any Cadillac limo) and bulky, the Countach feels and behaves rather like a racing sports car.

The well-equipped cabin carries wall-to-wall leather not only on the seat covers, but also on the sills and fascia, with a comprehensive display of instruments. Both a radio and air conditioning are standard.

On the other hand, there is no power assistance for the steering and no anti-lock braking. The wheels have different rim widths at front and rear (8.5 and 12 inches, respectively), with the Pirelli tires measuring no less than 345/35VR × 15 inches. This is serious, racing-standard stuff. And although the Countach *can* be driven quite slowly, it much prefers a life out on the open road, howling off toward distant horizons. Lamborghini might never have built true racing cars. Yet this supercar was, after all, conceived in race-mad Italy, and it delivers very strong cornering power indeed.

To stare at a Countach is to realize the absurdity of driving one in New York City. You can, on the other hand, imagine such a beast quartered at one's country house. There, it might be carefully fired up

*Scissor-action doors provide cockpit access, while other body panels lift to expose the mid-mounted V-12 and fore and aft cargo holds (**top**). About 150 Countachs are sold annually, a good number for the stratospheric price (**opposite page, top**). Ribbed air intakes in front of the wheel openings help identify this as the last Countach model before a replacement that's due in the early 1990s (**opposite page, bottom**). Chrysler Motors bought Lambo in 1987 and helped design the successor.*

# LAMBORGHINI JALPA

The causal observer may not be aware that Lamborghini had not one, but two supercars on sale in the late 1980s. In addition to the highly publicized and radically futuristic V-12 Countach, its V-8 powered brother found more than a few customers who craved a taste of Italian style and speed, but who would be content with an upper limit in the 145-mph neighborhood. Looking a bit more like a car than something out of *Star Wars*, the Lamborghini Jalpa gained a modest following among drivers who preferred an aggressive, manly body shape that suggested a kinship with high-

Ferruccio Lamborghini found fame with his V-12 GTs and supercars, but always wanted to produce a mid-engine V-8. The Italian automaker had little success with the 2+2 Urraco and 2-seat Silhouette in the 1970s before finding the right formula with the lively, aggressive-looking Jalpa in 1982 (**both pages**). Pronounced YAWL-pa, the pure 2-seater is styled by Bertone and uses a 250-horsepower 3.5-liter double overhead-cam V-8.

B990 HNV

# MERCEDES-BENZ 500SL

Rejecting the boulevard-cruiser image of its immediate predecessors, the 1990 500SL (**above**) has been cast by Mercedes-Benz as a true high-performance car. Despite the fat sticker price, the German automaker says the first two years of SL production sold out before the car's debut.

steel tubing that lies flush with the rear tonneau cover, ready to deploy in 0.3 seconds if various roll-angle, deceleration, and suspension-extension sensors detect signs of an impending flip. As a spring releases the roll bar, the seat belts tighten and the doors unlock. The roll bar works with either soft top or hardtop in place and can be slowly raised and lowered at will via a dashboard button. The windshield frame also is capable of providing some roll-over protection. Anti-lock brakes are standard and a traction-control system is to be offered on 1991 models.

The 500SL may not be nimble on the road, but it can thread purposely through thick traffic on its all-independent suspension and dig into most curves with an aplomb that belies its bulk. In sharp cornering or in very quick lane changes, however, the tail seems somewhat loose, suffering a mild swish where it should be sharp. The car's rear also will swing wide from rest under hard throttle. This brand of torque steer is testament to the V-8's power, which is always

Sequence at left shows manual deployment of the SL's roll-over bar; it springs up automatically in an emergency. SL is stable at 220 kilometers per hour— 137 mph (**top**). Functional side vents recall 1950s 300 SL (**above**). Removable aluminum hardtop is a standard feature and buttons up the roadster without harming its good looks (**opposite page**).

abundant, but never more so than above about 3000 rpm, where a press of the gas pedal is answered by a gush of acceleration. Although the power swells rather than explodes, the 500SL can nonetheless bound effortlessly past other cars at virtually any pace. In keeping with the policy of other German automakers to limit the top speed of their fastest cars, Mercedes has allowed the 500SL to top out at 155 mph, above which governors on fuel flow and other engine functions begin to retard speed. (Top speed in the 560SL was 139 mph.) At speed, the 500SL is impeccably stable, with a rock-solid bearing that exudes confidence as the car thunders by other traffic at well over 100 mph.

Overall comfort is very good, treading a middle ground between sportiness and refinement. Top down, the body quivers over cobblestones, but actual cowl shake or flexing of the structure escapes casual detection. Noise and wind levels at highway speeds are not enough to disrupt conversation. Mercedes offers what it calls the "draft stopper," a removable fabric panel designed to fit vertically behind the seats when the top is down. The panel decreases the volume of air rushing back into the cabin and makes the heater more effective. With the richly finished hard top fitted, the SL is noticeably more rigid and, as a bonus, loses none of its arresting good looks.

*At 322 horsepower, the 500SL's 5-liter dohc V-8 (**opposite page, top**) is one of the most powerful production engines available in the U.S. It propels the 4200-pound car to 60 mph in 6.2 seconds. Top speed would be about 170 mph, but a governor caps it at 155. Cabin is comfortable and sporty (**opposite page, bottom**). The 500SL loves high-speed straights and sweeping bends (**above**), though it acquits itself well on twisty roads.*

## Mercedes-Benz 500SL Major Specifications

**Manufacturer:**

Mercedes-Benz A.G., Stuttgart, West Germany

**Dimensions:**

| | |
|---|---|
| Wheelbase, in. | 99.0 |
| Overall length, in. | 176.0 |
| Overall width, in. | 71.3 |
| Overall height, in. | 51.2 |
| Track (front), in. | 60.3 |
| Track (rear), in. | 59.9 |
| Curb weight, lbs. | 4163 |

**Powertrain:**

| | |
|---|---|
| Layout: | front-engine, rear-wheel drive |
| Engine type: | double-overhead cam V-8 |
| Displacement, liters/cubic inches | 5.0/303 |
| Horsepower @ rpm | 322 @ 5500 |
| Torque (lbs./ft.) @ rpm | 332 @ 4000 |
| Fuel delivery: | Bosch KE 5 multi-port fuel injection |
| Transmission: | 4-speed automatic |

**Performance:**

| | |
|---|---|
| Top speed, mph | 155 |
| 0-60 mph, seconds | 6.2 |
| Quarter-mile, seconds | NA |

| | |
|---|---|
| **Approximate price:** | $80,000 |

# MERCEDES-BENZ/AMG HAMMER 6.0

Imagine hammering along Germany's speed-limitless Auto-bahn in your Ferrari Testarossa. Traffic's thin, you're feeling brave. You plant your Gucci firmly onto the accelerator. At around 176 mph, your prancing horse is in full stride and you, you're proud. But what's this? Headlights in your mirror? And gaining? They're flashing! You move right. A 4-door sedan slides by. Now that's hammering.

There's a fiendish one-upmanship in getting a utilitarian 5-passenger car to perform such deeds. And no one's more up on the game than a company called AMG, perhaps the world's most respected, successful, and imitated automotive modifier. Based in West Germany and with a branch in the U.S., AMG proves that Mercedes-Benz cars can be transformed into ultra-performance machines without compromising their considerable virtues as sedans and coupes. Nothing drives AMG's point home harder than its Hammer 6.0, essentially a luxury-laden Mercedes-Benz 300E capable of positively unholy performance: It can go 186 mph.

AMG gets the Mercedes to do that by resorting to the favorite trick of the American hot rodder: It drops in a bigger engine. Replacing the 300E's 3.0-liter inline six is the V-8 that powers the larger S-Class Mercedes sedans and coupe. AMG offers the standard-sized 5.6-liter

eight making 360 horsepower, or, for those with a lust for more go, a bored-out version displacing 6.0-liters and generating 375 horsepower. But size alone is not the story here.

AMG extracts from these engines much of their supercar bearing by replacing Mercedes' 2-valve cylinder heads with exquisite ported and polished 4-valve heads that incorporate special chain-driven twin camshafts. This essential hardware was designed by Erhard Melcher, who, along with engine builder Hans-Werner Aufrecht, established AMG in 1967. Aufrecht is the "A" in the company name, Melcher the "M"; the "G" is for Grossapach, Aurfrecht's birthplace. The pair toiled in the Mercedes factory competition shop before starting out on their own. They raced Mercedes and concentrated on engine building and suspension development until the late '70s. About 1978, they began to paint the cars in monochromatic color schemes. Complemented by their custom aerodynamic body add-ons and leading-edge wheel designs, the look swept the automotive universe. Trendy aftermarket stylists quickly picked it up and these days, even American automakers mimic the Euro cues and hues pioneered by AMG.

A full-dress Hammer 6.0 is indeed a dazzler. AMG paints all the trim, including the radiator grille, in body color, and lowers the car

AMG is perhaps the world's most respected, successful, and imitated automotive modifier. Its flagship is the Hammer 6.0 (**both pages**), a Mercedes-Benz 300E that's had its stock 177-horsepower 3-liter V-6 replaced by a highly modified 6-liter V-8 that churns out 375 horses and propels the 3600-pound sedan to 186 mph. Amazingly, the transformation does little to compromise the 300E's high level of refinement.

1.5 inches by tuning its standard 300E suspension for the rigors of ultra performance. A plastic air dam and side skirts add to the hunkered-down stance, while a steel rear-deck spoiler emphasizes the car's rakishness. Finishing the look are enormous polished chrome wheels of an AMG design. Eight inches wide, they carry Pirelli P700 tires, size 215/45VR17 in front, 235/45VR17 in the rear.

AMG has not neglected the interior, but unlike some European aftermarket firms, it shies away from new-wave digital instrumentation, wet bars, and television monitors. AMG sticks to black instrument faces with white markings—though some are modified for Hammer duty; the speedometer reads to 190 mph, for instance. Mercedes' bus-proportioned steering wheel is replaced by one of smaller diameter, the dashboard and door panels are treated to fine-wood inlays, and multi-position power leather-covered Recaro seats are installed.

AMG completes the package with such under-the-skin pieces as catalytic converters from the Porsche 928 S 4, ported intake and exhaust manifolds, a Mercedes automatic transmission fortified to handle the extra power, a Gleason-Torsen limited slip differential, and a 2.24:1 final-drive ratio. Taken as a whole, the Hammer is one slick power tool.

AMG pioneered the use of aerodynamic body add-ons and monochromatic paint schemes (**opposite page**) that swept the world of high-fashion automobiles and trickled down even to Detroit-made compact cars. Finishing the Look on the Hammer 6.0 are polished chrome wheels of an AMG design (**below**). Eight inches wide, they carry Pirelli P700 tires, size 215/45VR17 in front, 235/45VR17 at the rear.

Its engine starts without fuss and will run all day without a stumble. Acceleration is linear and uninterrupted. The power seems to gush from some bottomless reservoir, whether leaping away from a standstill or rocketing ahead from 80 mph. The tires and suspension keep the car buttoned down at speed and help it conquer corners with aplomb. The Hammer takes bumps with slightly more stiffness than the stock 300E, but the legendary Mercedes ability to absorb dips and pavement irregularities with world-class control, especially at speed, is undiminished. AMG retains intact Mercedes' speed-sensitive power steering and its 4-wheel anti-lock disc brakes. Both work flawlessly. The Hammer isn't twitchy above 130, and can be hauled back to mortal-car speeds with confidence-inspiring predictability.

That's a lot of goodness, but then the AMG Hammer costs a lot of money. Various V-8 engine, trim, and accessory combinations are available, but none can be had for much under $130,000. The Hammer 6.0 flagship sedan goes for $165,000. For that you get stratospheric levels of performance in a car that's easy to get into and out of, that offers the driver excellent visibility and comfort, and one that can carry five people and their luggage. AMG's workmanship and materials are of Mercedes-Benz quality—what higher level is there? Even at the price, in the out-of-this-world world of exotic cars, the Hammer is actually a bargain. It may not look as swoopy as the typical mid-engine 2-seater, but it's faster than most, and easier to live with than all of them. The Hammer may not wow the masses, but it certainly will impress those most worth impressing.

*Big Mercedes V-8 is a tight squeeze in the 300E's engine bay (**opposite page, top**). AMG replaces the stock 2-valve cylinder heads with ported and polished 4-valve heads of its own design. Inside, AMG shies away from gimmickry in favor of modifications that emphasize class and function (**opposite page, bottom**). Taken as a whole, the Hammer 6.0 (**above**) is one slick power tool.*

### Mercedes-Benz/AMG Hammer 6.0
### Major Specifications

**Manufacturer:**

Mercedes-Benz A.G.; Stuttgart, Germany. Engine, suspension, interior and exterior modifications by AMG of North America; Westmont, Illinois.

**Dimensions:**

| | |
|---|---|
| Wheelbase, in. | 110.2 |
| Overall length, in. | 186.6 |
| Overall width, in. | 68.5 |
| Overall height, in. | 54.1 |
| Track (front), in. | 58.9 |
| Track (rear), in. | 58.6 |
| Curb weight, lbs. | 3635 |

**Powertrain:**

| | |
|---|---|
| Layout: | front-engine, rear-wheel drive |
| Engine type: | double overhead-cam V-8 |
| Displacement, liters/cubic inches | 6.0/363 |
| Horsepower @ rpm | 375 @ 5500 |
| Torque (lbs./ft.) @ rpm | est. 400 @ 4000 |
| Fuel delivery: | Bosch K-Jetronic fuel injection |
| Transmission: | 4-speed automatic |

**Performance:**

| | |
|---|---|
| Top speed, mph | 186 |
| 0-60 mph, seconds | 5.2 |
| Quarter-mile, seconds | 13.6 |

| | |
|---|---|
| **Approximate price:** | $165,000 |

# NISSAN GTP ZX-TURBO

**N**ot every element of Nissan's super-swift IMSA racing car hails from the land of the rising sun. Its body is British, its engineering and crew is Californian. But the twin turbocharged 3-liter V-6 GTP ZX-Turbocars deliver 780 horsepower, plenty enough to make a major impression on any track in the world. Don Devendorf's team at Electramotive Engineering in El Segundo, California, has figured out the arcane art of winning prototype races on the Camel GT circuit.

The Nissan GTP cars are rarely the fastest of the lot, however. Their technology is expressed not in high speeds but, in sensational lap times. Road races are won in the corners. And with the Nissan a second or two quicker through the twisty bits, the car's technological edge resulted in a record-setting 1988 string of overall victories, track records, and pole positions. Yet the ZX-Turbo didn't vault to prominence immediately.

In today's highly sophisticated IMSA prototype racing, which is contested on some 15 different tracks, there is no single perfect chassis to "dial in" for victory. Conditions change constantly. Track surfaces heat up and cool down, become slippery with rubber and oil. Decreasing fuel loads reduce a car's weight and change handling characteristics. Add engine tune and fuel management; front and rear suspension setup; bodywork, wings, and tabs; the trade-off of down force and aerodynamic drag; underbody air movement. It's a multitude of intertwined parameters that weave a web of near-infinite variation.

The Nissan ZX-Turbo (**both pages**) began its racing career in 1985, but success was at first elusive. However, a chassis by Trevor Harris and subsequent development in a ground-plane wind tunnel helped make it competitive. By 1988, the ZX-Turbo was winning—and setting track records.

# OLDSMOBILE AEROTECH

On November 16, 1986, at the General Motors Desert Proving Ground in Mesa, Arizona, the American automobile industry entered a new age. On its shake-down cruise, with a significantly detuned engine, the Oldsmobile Aerotech research vehicle recorded an average lap speed of 218.44 mph.

That was just the beginning. This record-setting car would go on to demonstrate that an American automaker had the ability to plan and to build a car as advanced—and as fast—as any in the world. Officially, the goal of GM's Aerotech program was to evaluate Oldsmobile's new 16-valve, double-overhead cam Quad 4 engine at its highest levels of performance. Unofficially, Olds was out to punch a few headline-grabbing holes in the world's closed-course speed record.

Thanks to an international team of designers and technicians, plus the talents of one of America's foremost race drivers, the Aerotech emerged not only as a remarkable engineering triumph, but as a styling achievement.

It started with a concept. On February 14, 1984, Oldsmobile chief engineer Theodore N. Louckes established the initial objective: Build a high speed vehicle for the Quad 4. That simple goal spawned a mountain of questions: Who would build the chassis? Which body design would be used? How aerodynamic would it have to be? How much power could the little 2.3-liter Quad 4 produce? Who would drive the car? Which records should be chased?

Just three weeks after Louckes laid down the initial plans at Oldsmobile's Lansing headquarters, another discussion took place in Houston, Texas. At issue was whether the Aerotech could break then-current lap records at the Indianapolis Motor Speedway (217.581 mph) and at NASCAR's Alabama International Motor Speedway in Talladega (221 mph). The man Louckes' team selected to find out was none other than America's most versatile driver, builder, and racing manager, A.J. Foyt.

On March 27 representatives from each of the major suppliers to the Aerotech project met with the GM design staff at the GM Tech Center in Warren, Michigan. Batten Engineering was there for engine development; March Engineering for its chassis expertise; and GM design staff for support. The GM Aerodynamics Lab was to play a key role, as was Oldsmobile Engineering. An artist's conception of the car came from Ed Welburn of the GM Design Staff. Foyt Enterprises was to supply on-track development and Anthony Joseph Foyt himself would drive the car. Coordinating the effort was Bill Porterfield, an Oldsmobile future systems and technology engineer, who was named manager of the Aerotech and Super Heavy Duty (SHD) Quad 4 development program.

*Built to highlight Oldsmobile engine technology, the Aerotech just happened to shatter some speed records along the way. The long-tail car (**above**) blistered the asphalt at 278 mph on the way to a 267-mph flying-mile record. The short tail car (**opposite page**) set the world's closed-course speed record of 257 mph.*

Aerotech eventually became two cars of slightly different shapes tailored to their slightly different purposes. Both were the product of the design staff's Welburn, a racing driver fascinated with the low-drag cars used in ultra high-speed competition at Le Mans. His work on production cars had involved the Cutlass Supreme and Cutlass Ciera and Calais, but he had found time to sketch his dream car, a truly high-performance Oldsmobile. When Olds engineers approached the GM Design Staff to develop a car blending aerodynamic form with engineering function, they found Welburn's rendering on casual display in his studio. This was the car they were looking for. Welburn's dream was about to come true. The Aerotech evolved very much along the lines Welburn had sketched. Its original full-size mock-up took shape in secrecy in the basement of the GM Design Staff building.

Building the full-size Aerotech body of carbon fiber panels stretched design knowledge. "The area where the radiator and intercooler inlets and exits are located was an enormous challenge for the guys making the molds," Welburn said. "That was probably the most difficult area."

Once the shape of the car was established, Austrian-born GM staff project engineer Franz K. (Max) Schenkel became instrumental in fine tuning the Aerotech for aerodynamic efficiency. The car was divided into upper and lower body segments. Schenkel built 1/3-scale and full size models to establish the vehicle's low-drag characteristics and played a major role in developing the car's innovative adjustable underbody tunnels used to create downforce. The finished design is 40 inches high, 86 inches wide, and 192 inches long. In final form, says Welburn, "The upper body shape really did not change much at all. It was low drag from the beginning." By September of 1984, Schenkel had determined the horsepower needed to set new speed records with the Aerotech shape.

Beneath the skin is a March Engineering chassis fitted with a single turbocharger Quad 4 developed by Batten Engineering. This engine, designated the Super Heavy Duty "RE," retains the street Quad 4's

Ed Welburn was a member of the General Motors design staff and a racing driver fascinated with the low-drag cars used in ultra high-speed competition at LeMans. Olds engineers happened to see Welburn's rendering of an aero Olds dreamcar on casual display in his studio. This was what they were looking for and the Aerotech cars (**left**) evolved very much along the lines Welburn had sketched. The original full-size mock-up took shape in secrecy in the GM design staff basement.

Beneath Aerotech's carbon fiber skin is a March Engineering chassis fitted with a highly developed turbocharged Olds dohc 4-cylinder engine (**above**). This engine (**right**) retains the street Quad 4's aluminum alloy block, combustion-chamber shape, valve angle and sizes, chain driven camshafts, electronic fuel injection, and integrated direct-fire ignition. Unlike the maximum 180 horsepower generated by its street cousin, however, the Aerotech's Quad 4 puts out up to 1000 horsepower. That's how driver A.J. Foyt was able to deliver a very unstreetlike 250-plus mph (**opposite page**).

100-mm bore spacing in an aluminum alloy block cast by Batten. Quad 4 combustion-chamber shape is retained, as is valve angle and size, chain driven camshafts, electronic fuel injection, and integrated direct-fire ignition. Proof that true high speeds were within reach was established when Foyt wheeled the short-tail Aerotech #2 onto GM's Desert Proving Grounds and took it up to 218 mph.

By the following March (1987), the twin turbocharged Quad 4, designated the "BE", was running on the dyno. This was the engine for Aerotech #1, the long-tail car. The body shape of this car was developed for increased down force on tracks with tighter turns, such as Indianapolis, rather than the gently sweeping 5-mile oval at GM's Mesa proving grounds or the 7.7-mile test track at Ft. Stockton, Texas.

On July 28, 1987, Foyt evaluated the short-tail Aerotech at Ft. Stockton. He recorded a 227 mph average lap speed with a scorching 241 mph straightaway speed. There was no doubt about it, Aerotech could set land speed records.

To Ft. Stockton on August 27, Foyt brought his four Indianapolis 500 wins, his Le Mans 24-Hour victory, his Daytona 500 win, and his lifetime of racing and winning with about every type of road and track racing car of modern times. Olds engineering brought their Aerotechs.

With USAC and ACCUS certifying the attempts, Foyt brought the world's closed-course speed record back to the USA. His 257.123 mph with the Aerotech ST (Short Tail) bested the 250.918 mph record set in Nardo, Italy during 1979 by a dual turbocharged V-8 Mercedes-Benz. It also erased the 1986 closed-course record of 233.934 mph set by Rick Mears in a Turbocharged Chevrolet Ilmor V-8 Indycar at Michigan International Speedway.

The awesome Texan then burned the Aerotech LT (Long Tail) into the record books with a new "flying mile" average speed record of 267.399 mph. That smashed the old record by more than 12 mph. To establish his "average" speed Foyt actually reached a blistering 278.357 mph on one pass.

## Oldsmobile Aerotech Major Specifications

**Manufacturer:**

Oldsmobile Division, General Motors; Lansing, Michigan

**Dimensions:**

| | |
|---|---|
| Wheelbase, in. | 111.3 |
| Overall length, in. | 192.0 |
| Overall width, in. | 86.0 |
| Overall height, in. | 40.1 |
| Track (front), in. | 66.0 |
| Track (rear), in. | 63.0 |
| Curb weight, lbs. | 1600 |

**Powertrain:**

| | |
|---|---|
| Layout: | mid-engine, rear-wheel drive |
| Engine type: | turbocharged double-overhead-cam inline 4-cylinder |
| Displacement, liters/cubic inches | 2.0/122 |
| Horsepower @ rpm | 800-1000 @ 9500 |
| Torque (lbs./ft.) @ rpm | NA |
| Fuel delivery: | electronic fuel injection |
| Transmission: | 6-speed ZF manual |

**Performance:**

| | |
|---|---|
| Top speed, mph | 257.1 (ST); 267.4 (LT) |
| 0-60 mph, seconds | NA |
| Quarter-mile, seconds | est. 8.1 |

| | |
|---|---|
| **Approximate price:** | NA |

# 20TH ANNIVERSARY PONTIAC TURBO TRANS AM

nniversary models often deliver a lot more show than go, and sometimes not much of either. Pontiac's 20th Anniversary Turbo Trans Am dishes up both. It combines the standard Trans Am's assertive lines with a meaner demeanor. Pontiac's claim to "build excitement" has seldom been truer for any car. Its 20th Anniversary TA is at once sophisticated and a throwback to the days of the fastest pony cars. If you enjoy being shoved back hard in your seat as the gas pedal goes down, a Turbo TA is eager to comply.

The car celebrates a model that was added almost as an afterthought by Pontiac back in 1969. Firebird actually hit the market for the 1967 model year. Sharing the same body and platform with Chevrolet's Camaro, Firebirds found 82,560 buyers in that first season. America's late-1960s mania for rapid street cars spawned a host of tough models from Pontiac, including a flock of Firebirds. Through 1969, the hottest Firebird was the Firebird 400 Ram Air IV, with its 400-cubic-inch V-8 rated at 345 horsepower. Pony-car performance was oriented mostly toward straight-line acceleration in those days, but in March

of '69, Pontiac introduced a new model that looked for inspiration toward the exciting Sports Car Club of America Trans-American Sedan Series of road races. The Firebird Trans Am was unveiled with little fanfare—no consumer literature on the car was even published. That first Trans Am was little more than a stripe-and-scoop cosmetic treatment of a Firebird 400 and just 697 were built. It was, nonetheless, the birth one of the most important cars in Pontiac history.

Along with the Camaro, Firebird was rebodied for 1970 with a design that would become a modern-day classic. The Trans Am, with sharp-edged air dams and spoilers accentuating the new body's sensuous curves, was clearly the top-dog Firebird now. It would continue as such, always with the biggest, baddest Firebird engines and best suspension pieces. The third-generation Firebird and Camaro debuted for 1982 with aerodynamic drag coefficients as low as 0.309. They were some of the best wind cheaters ever produced for public consumption. By this time, brute horsepower had given way to balanced handling, bigger tires, and better brakes, but the Trans Am

The tough-guy aero look and gorgeous BBS-style lattice-work alloy wheels of the Firebird GTA aren't enough for the 20th Anniversary Trans Am (**both pages**). It can also boast "Official Pace Car" status on its doors. Gaudy, sure, but plant your right foot and you'll snatch the smile right off the face of the snickerer in the next lane. Wait an instant for the big Garrett T3 intercooled turbocharger to spool up and the Anniversary TA launches itself like an attack jet catapulted from the USS Nimitz. Conservatively rated at 250 horsepower, the 3.8-liter V-6 pulls strongly all the way past 140 mph, where the TA remains quite stable as long as the pavement stays smooth.

mystique was undiminished.

The fuel crunch of 1979 forced Pontiac to abandon its large-displacement V-8s. The largest offered in a Firebird for '79 was a 301-cubic-incher. Available on the Trans Am and Formula models was Firebird's first turbocharged engine, a 210-horsepower version of the 301. The 1980 Turbo TA was the first Trans Am to pace the Indianapolis 500. Pontiac boasted that the only major modification for Speedway duty was removal of the air conditioning system. But in 1989, Pontiac would unleash a Trans Am so capable that leading 33 of the world's fastest race cars around the Indy track would, in fact, require no modifications at all.

The 20th Anniversary Trans Am that paced the '89 Indy 500 is derived from the V-8 powered Firebird GTA. It went on sale in mid-'89 in a limited-edition of just 1500. All are identical, all painted white, and all officially qualify as pace cars, since each one meets every Speedway performance requirement.

Firebirds had used V-6 engines before. But they were nothing like the 3.8-liter unit in the Anniversary car. The engine had made its mark in the Buick Regal Grand National, which brought the curtain down on the big, rear-drive Detroit muscle car in a tire-smoking blaze of glory. Though the GN was retired at the end of the '88 model year, there were still some 245-horsepower turbocharged 3.8 engines in the General Motors inventory. Happily, they fit in the Firebird.

Armed with a Garrett T3 intercooled turbocharger, the 20th Anniversary 3.8 V-6 is rated at 250 horsepower and 340 pounds/feet of torque. GM's 700R4 HydraMatic 4-speed automatic is the only transmission offered. The combination of 0.7:1 overdrive 4th, plus a limited-slip rear axle of 3.27:1 final drive, produces an ultra-low

The first turbocharged Trans Am appeared in 1979 with a 301-cubic-inch V-8 rated at 210 horsepower. The '80 turbo was the first TA to pace the Indy 500. Unlike that model, however, the 20th Anniversary turbo TA that paced the 1989 race didn't have to be hopped up to meet the Speedway's acceleration, braking, and top speed requirements. Pontiac simply plucked one from the production run of 1500; the only modification was the addition of a safety flashing-light bar on the roof.

2.289:1 overall ratio. Normal road speeds are accomplished at a lazy rpm, little more than twice idle speed. On the low end, the tranny's violent 3.06:1 first-gear ratio can roast the rear rubber with little provocation. Comparing 0-60 mph times, the GTA, with its 235-horsepower 5.7-liter V-8, falls in the 7-second range, while the Turbo V-6 rockets to 60 in a vein-popping 5.3 seconds. Given the road, a 20th Anniversary Trans Am will touch 150 mph.

The aerodynamic Indian moves quickly in more ways than one. Even at a list price of more than $29,000, it was an almost immediate sellout. External identification of the Turbo TA includes a "20th Anniversary" insignia on the nose and sail panel. "GTA" script on front fenders, just behind the wheel well arch, is replaced by "Turbo Trans Am" lettering. Each car displays a special Indianapolis Motor Speedway logo in a cloisonne emblem attached to both right and left lower rocker panels, ahead of the doors. Every buyer of the 20th edition Trans Am also receives a complete set of official Indianapolis 500 Pace Car decals for both the door and windshield.

This Pontiac is no Porsche in the turns, but it does well enough with anti-sway bars front and rear, 4-wheel anti-lock disc brakes, and Goodyear Eagle ZR50-series Gatorbacks rated for over 149 mph. The car's 0.84 g skidpad lateral acceleration exceeds that of the Lotus Esprit (0.82 g). Not too shabby for a car that traces its origins to an unheralded mid-year addition to the Firebird line.

*The 20th Anniversary Trans Am is plagued by creaks from its T-tops and a buckboard ride, but all is forgiven once the throttle opens. Few cars feel as untamed on the street. The cabin (**opposite page, top**) carries full GTA instrumentation, including sound-system controls in the steering-wheel hub. A 4-speed overdrive automatic is the only available transmission. The hot V-6 engine (**left**) is taken from the legendary Buick Grand National.*

## Pontiac 20th Anniversary Trans Am Major Specifications

**Manufacturer:**

Pontiac Motor Division, General Motors Corporation, Pontiac, Michigan; and PAS Inc.; City of Industry, California

**Dimensions:**

| | |
|---|---|
| Wheelbase, in. | 101.0 |
| Overall length, in. | 191.6 |
| Overall width, in. | 72.4 |
| Overall height, in. | 50.0 |
| Track (front), in. | 60.7 |
| Track (rear), in. | 61.6 |
| Curb weight, lbs. | 3468 |

**Powertrain:**

| | |
|---|---|
| Layout: | front-engine, rear-wheel drive |
| Engine type: | turbocharged, intercooled overhead-valve V-6 |
| Displacement, liters/cubic inches | 3.8/231 |
| Horsepower @ rpm | 250 @ 4400 |
| Torque (lbs./ft.) @ rpm | 340 @ 2800 |
| Fuel delivery: | port fuel injection |
| Transmission: | 4-speed automatic |

**Performance:**

| | |
|---|---|
| Top speed, mph | 150 |
| 0-60 mph, seconds | 5.3 |
| Quarter-mile, seconds | 13.9 |

| **Approximate price:** | $29,839 |
|---|---|

# PONTIAC NASCAR GRAND PRIX

**R**usty Wallace honed his driving edge on the dust-bowl circuits of the midwest for nearly eight years before bursting upon the NASCAR scene in 1980 with a 2nd-place finish in the Atlanta 500. It was his very first NASCAR drive. The rising star joined the Blue Max Pontiac team in '85, and by '88, was after nothing less than a Winston Cup Championship. He opened the season behind the wheel of an all-new—and unproven—car. By the final race of the season, the tow-haired charger with the hard, clear eyes would know a lot more about his new Grand Prix, and a lot more about what it means to be a champion.

Nineteen eighty-eight was the year General Motors transformed the popular Pontiac from a boxy, rear-drive 2-door sedan into a sleek, front-drive coupe. The new car's shape seemed well-suited to slicing through the air. But nothing can substitute for real-world competition and NASCAR teams over the years had developed the previous GM

Like all modern NASCAR stockers, Rusty Wallace's Pontiac Grand Prix (**both pages**) is really only a thin metal shell that looks like its production counterpart. Underneath is a high-tech and ultra-strong roll cage/chassis. This frame forms a rigid platform for an adjustable racing suspension and a rear-drive powertrain pulled along by a roaring V-8 engine (**opposite page, bottom**). The intent is safety and speed—if the two can be synonymous at more than 200 mph.

body into an enormously effective racing machine.

Once on the track, though, the more tapered '88 Grand Prix indeed had less aerodynamic drag, and, as it turned out, was a better balanced, better handling racer. But it took Wallace a while to adapt to the new car. When he finally did, nothing could touch him.

Like all modern NASCAR stockers, Wallace's Grand Prix is really only a thin metal shell that looks like its production counterpart. Underneath is a high-tech and ultra-strong roll cage/chassis. This frame forms a rigid platform for an adjustable racing suspension and a rear-drive powertrain pulled along by a roaring V-8 engine. The intent is safety and speed—if the two can be synonymous at more than 200 mph.

Mike and Jack Laughlin of Simpsonville, South Carolina, are chassis constructors for the Blue Max Pontiacs, a squadron of Grand Prixs consisting of three superspeedway cars, a trio of short trackers, and a road racer. Bodywork and remaining assembly are done in-house by the Blue Max team. The primary difference between the Blue Max cars is their weight distribution and tread width. A Jerico 4-speed transmission is preferred for road racing, a Tex Enterprises T-10 is used in oval-track cars. On the long tracks, the cars are fitted with 3.10:1 final drive gearing. On short tracks, they run with a 5.29 gear.

Intermediate-size tracks are run with a 4.22:1 final-drive ratio. Four-wheel disc brakes and 15-inch wheels are used for all tracks.

NASCAR rules set minimum weight at 3500 pounds for Winston Cup cars. On lower-speed short-track cars, a 50/50 weight distribution is the norm. On the giant ovals, a 53/47 mix adds weight out front to hold the cars down at high speeds, limit air turbulence underneath, and promote arrow-like straight-line stability.

Though NASCAR rules governing Winston Cup engines are stringent, each engine builder has a bag of tricks designed to coax from the engine the monstrous power and stamina required to compete. The Blue Max team Pontiac, and most other General Motors superspeedway cars, run engines of 14:1 compression ratio built from the legendary 350-cubic-inch Chevrolet small-block V-8. A typical engine is good for 635 unrestricted horsepower at 7800 rpm. An 830-cfm Holley 4-barrel is used to keep the torque peak high in the rev band. At Daytona and Talladega, where NASCAR requires a carburetor-restriction plate, horsepower is reduced to about 500. Engines used on the short tracks run carburetors of around 750 cfm, which allows them to generate maximum torque at lower rpm.

Neither engine builders nor the drivers like artificially restricted power, but the NASCAR rules committee seems to think that reducing airflow into an engine reduces top speeds. What really happens is several cars draft in a line. Drop out of line and the aerodynamic brakes come on, pushing a car back several places. It's this kind of dicey racing that makes today's Winston Cup circuit so demanding to drive and so exciting to watch. Throw in the tail-out high jinks rewarded on the short tracks and the deft touch called for on the road courses, and it's easy to see why a Pontiac Grand Prix in the hands of a driver of Wallace's diverse background is such a threat.

Steaming out of the Missouri hamlet of Fenton (population, 2400), Wallace won 202 races on the hard-scrabble American Speed Association (ASA) circuit. He was the United States Auto Club 1979 Stock Car Rookie of the Year and 1983 ASA stock-car champion. Wallace came to NASCAR for good in '84, winning Champion Spark Plug Rookie of the Year honors with the Cliff Stewart Racing team.

Wallace moved into the driver's seat of the Blue Max Pontiacs in 1985. The Blue Max contingent was formed during the '82 season by Raymond Beadle, a six-time drag racing world champion from Dallas. At its center is engine man Harold Elliott, who learned his tricks building motors for Junior Johnson, among other stock-car heros.

Wallace notched his first Winston Cup victory in the 1986 Valleydale 500 at Bristol. He won another short-track race that year and finished 5th in points. He proved his road-race acumen in '87, taking the checkered in both the 500-miler at Watkins Glen and the Winston Western 500 at Riverside. Wallace ran with the leaders often in '87, but again finished 5th in points overall. Now respected as a hard charger, Wallace entered the '88 season counting on his white and green Kodiak/Mobile 1 Pontiac for four or five wins and the Winston Cup title.

Teething problems with the new car kept Wallace out of the win column until June 12, when he finished first on Riverside's road course. He won at Michigan two weeks later, but didn't see victory lane again until October 9, at Charlotte. Meanwhile, points leader Bill Elliott was notching four wins. With season's end in sight, Wallace's dream of a Winston Cup crown was fading. They got no brighter when Elliott qualified on the pole at North Wilkesboro. But Wallace drove tough and won the race. Next came Rockingham, with Elliott again on the pole. But it was Wallace who snared the win.

No doubt about it, the Grand Prix finally was working. There had been a season-long debate about the aerodynamics of the new

*NASCAR rules set a minimum weight of 3500 pounds for Winston Cup cars like the Grand Prix (**left**). On lower-speed, short-track cars, a 50/50 weight distribution is the norm. On the giant ovals, a 53/47 mix adds ballast out front to hold the cars down at high speeds, limit air turbulence underneath, and promote straight-line stability.*

216

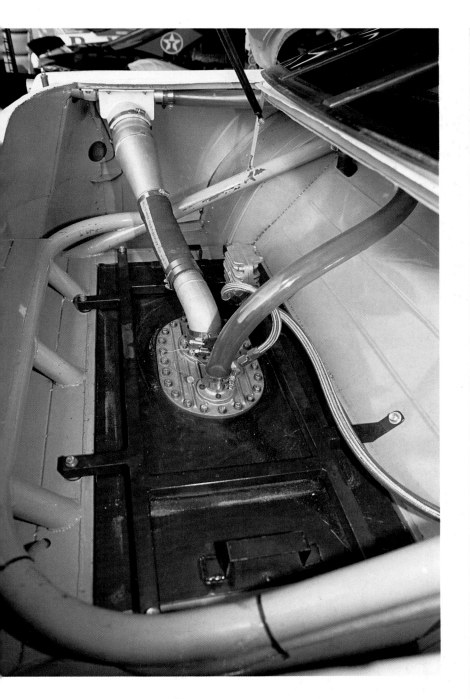

body shape, but when Wallace dove at will under Dale Earnhardt's Chevrolet, the crew knew it had found the right setup. Wallace was raking in the points, and by the Miller 400 on the brand-new ¾-mile track at Richmond, he was only 26 points behind Elliott. Then, disaster. Wallace slowed under a yellow flag, but Geoff Bodine whacked the Blue Max Kodiak/Mobile 1 Grand Prix. The shunt sent the car to the garage and pushed Wallace 119 points back of Elliott.

But Wallace wasn't about to concede. A showdown would take place in the last race of the year, the Atlanta Journal 500 at the Atlanta International Raceway, Elliott's "home" track. Wallace was inspired and his Grand Prix was untouchable. He seized the pole at a record qualifying speed of 174.499 mph. He led the race early, then fell a lap down after blowing a tire. Charging hard now, Wallace unlapped himself, moved back into contention, and grabbed the lead again. In all, he led four times, 166 of the 328 laps. Wallace was dominating. But Elliott was wily.

Ahead on points, Awesome Bill had only to finish 18th to clinch the Winston Cup championship. Elliott feathered his Ford Thunderbird, hanging loose around mid-pack, never challenging, never pressing. He coasted home, 11 places behind race winner Wallace, but in front on points by 24. Final Winston Cup tally: Elliott, six wins, six poles, 4488 points; Wallace six wins (three of the last four races), two poles, 4464 points. It was the narrowest championship margin since Earnhardt nipped Cale Yarborough by 19 points in 1980.

Wallace was livid. "I had to go hard from the start, but (Elliott) could just ease along. I had to throw everything I had at him. We did everything we could do, but we just came up short . . . . That 24-point difference is killing me. I'm a terrible loser." Terrible losers one year make wonderful winners the next.

Gasoline is gravity fed into a racing-spec fuel cell nestled in the Grand Prix's trunk area (**opposite page, top, and left**). Rising star Wallace (**opposite page, bottom**) believes NASCAR champions must always drive hard. Rear spoiler (**bottom**) can be adjusted for size and angle to achieve the best aerodynamics on each track.

## Pontiac NASCAR Grand Prix
## Major Specifications

### Manufacturer:
Blue Max Racing Inc., Charlotte, N.C.

### Dimensions:

| | |
|---|---:|
| Wheelbase, in. | 110.0 |
| Overall length, in. | 193.9 |
| Overall width, in. | 69.0 |
| Overall height, in. | 50.5 |
| Track (front), in. | 59.0 |
| Track (rear), in. | 59.0 |
| Curb weight, lbs. | 3500 |

### Powertrain:

| | |
|---|---:|
| Layout: | front-engine, rear drive |
| Engine type: | overhead valve V-8 (aluminum heads) |
| Displacement, liters/cubic inches | NA/358 |
| Horsepower @ rpm | 640 @ 7800 |
| Torque (lbs./ft.) @ rpm | 480 @ 7800 |
| Fuel delivery: | 830 cfm or 750 cfm 4-barrel carburetor |
| Transmission: | (oval tracks) Borg-Warner T-10 4-speed manual (road courses) Jerico 4-speed |

### Performance:

| | |
|---|---:|
| Top speed, mph | 215 |
| 0-60 mph, seconds | NA |
| Quarter-mile, seconds | est. 7.5 |

### Approximate Price: $80,000

# PORSCHE 911 CARRERA 4

The 911 Carrera 4 (**below**) builds upon the rear-engine layout and sensuously curved body of the classic 911, but updates it with a powerful new engine, refined aerodynamics, power steering, anti-lock brakes, a new climate-control system, and most significantly, a sophisticated all-wheel drive system. The result, say some very tough critics, is "the best supercar money can buy."

In 1987, Porsche's vision of the future was glimpsed by only 200 or so souls fortunate enough to acquire its ground-breaking, all-wheel-drive 959. In 1989, Porsche opened wide the window to tomorrow with mass production of its 911 Carrera 4.

A slew of manufacturers sell 4-wheel drive performance automobiles. But the 911 Carrera 4 comes from the world's slickest sports-car maker. It should be the standard by which others are judged. Is it?

To the disappointment of some, the car looks almost exactly like the 911 models churned out of Zuffenhausen since way back in 1963. And, indeed, the dimensions are virtually identical, even though the Carrera 4 is built on an all-new floorpan. The similarity in size and appearance is quite intentional, says Porsche: The 911 design is a classic, a symbol of Porsche itself, the one unbroken thread in the proud company's rich automotive tapestry. In fact, the Carrera 4 is a touchstone both to Porsche's past and its future. It's the foundation of a whole new generation of naturally aspirated and turbocharged, 2- and 4-wheel drive 911 coupes and cabriolets that will take the company well into the 21st Century. And even though the Carrera 4 retains the 911's iconoclastic rear-engine layout, it shares only 15 percent of its parts—mostly outer-body panels—with the previous 911 series.

Actually, subtle changes to the 911's front and rear aprons and bumpers, plus the addition of a full-length belly pan, make the Carrera 4 much more aerodynamic than the previous 911. Its drag coefficient is down to 0.32, from the base 911's 0.39. To maintain the clean rear slope of the 911's body, Porsche equipped the Carrera 4 with an extendable rear spoiler that deploys automatically at about 50 mph and retracts automatically at about 6 mph. In addition to enhancing high-speed stability, the extended spoiler nearly doubles the size of the air intake grille for the Carrera's hot new engine.

Porsche chose to debut in the Carrera 4 the most powerful normally aspirated engine ever offered in a 911. The evergreen Porsche flat-six design is retained, but displacement is increased from 3.2-liters to 3.6. New cylinder heads incorporate twin-spark plug ignition adapted from Porsche's PFM 3200 aircraft engine. The result is 247 horsepower, good enough to send the 3200-pound coupe to 60 mph in 5.3 seconds and to a top speed of 162 mph. Now encapsulated for better noise isolation, the flat six is indeed quieter, but little of the glorious Porsche 911 sound has been lost.

There is one 911 trait the Carrera is designed not to retain, however. Tail-heavy and very powerful, the rear-engine, rear-wheel-drive 911 makes even experienced drivers timid with its propensity to spin stern-first off the road if the throttle is lifted in mid-corner or if too much gas is applied coming out of a fast turn.

The Carrera 4 seeks to tame this behavior with a sophisticated 4-wheel drive system that responds automatically to changing road conditions and driving situations. Unlike the Porsche 959, the Carrera 4 doesn't require the driver to select a torque-split program appropriate for road conditions. In normal operation, 31 percent of the Carrera 4's engine power goes to the front wheels and 69 percent to the rear. Wheel-spin sensors in the anti-lock braking system—the Carrera 4 is the first 911 with ABS—lookout for a loss of traction by monitoring both lateral and longitudinal forces and differences in rotational speed of the wheels. The sensors can recognize wheel-speed variations as small as .6 mph. When a tire slips in acceleration or in a turn, the center and rear differentials are hydraulically engaged and disengaged as needed to feed power to the axle with the best traction. Response time for engagement is less than one-tenth of a second, three times faster than 959 system. Thresholds are set so that minor differences in wheel speed, such as in very tight corners, will not cause unnecessary engagement. For really slippery surfaces, like snow-covered inclines, the driver can turn a console-mounted traction switch to lock both differentials.

Similarly, the Carrera 4's suspension is an advancement over that of the 911's. The 911's torsion bars are replaced by coil springs both front and rear. In back, a semi-trailing arm provides rear toe correction in cornering, an effect similar to that of the Weissach axle on the 928 S4.

Professional road testers are unanimous in their praise of the Carrera 4's powertrain, though some complain of engine noise on long trips and of the heavy clutch action. Others criticize the Carrera 4's ride as too harsh. The new car introduces to the 911 family power steering that's supremely accurate, but some testers miss the unadulterated precision and kick-back of the 911's manual steering. And while this is the first 911 designed with air conditioning in mind, rare is the driver who sees the revamped Carrera 4 dashboard as any real improvement over the old 911's.

All-wheel drive means all-weather dexterity for the Carrera 4. Porsche's system was pioneered on the 1983 959 concept car (**opposite page, inset**), though the Carrera 4's setup actually is more user friendly. Extended spoiler increases engine-air intake grille by nearly 50 percent (**above**).

222

New 3.6-liter flat six (**opposite page, bottom**) uses Porsche aircraft technology. The rear spoiler extends automatically at over 50 mph (**opposite page, top**), retracts at under 6 mph (**above**). New shifter and a revamped dashboard with better air conditioning mark the Carrera 4's cabin (**top**).

But these are hardened road testers, many of whom have been bitten in the past by the bad manners of the 2-wheel drive 911. When they do what they can to mimic its worst behavior in the Carrera 4, they find that they cannot. And there is joy.

"Porsche fixes the 911," happily declares *Automobile Magazine*. "On little D-numbered roads in France's south-coastal mountains above Nice and Cannes, the Carrera 4 safely maintained astounding speeds, slithering and pattering over pavement ranging from glassy to ghastly."

Closer to home, *Car and Driver*'s brisk run through the Ohio outback revealed that "Remarkably stable, wickedly fast, and astoundingly easy to drive, this 911 comes as a pointed fist in the face of doubters. . . . Here at last is a finely conceived, exquisitely built, ruggedly rocketlike German sports car that redefines the delivery of all-out road performance via four-wheel drive."

Yet, some veterans mourn that the 911's sense of immediacy has been dulled in the Carrera 4.

"Is the Carrera 4 as much fun, on the tighter roads, as a normal 911?" asked Britain's *Car* magazine. "No, in all honesty, it probably is not." ". . . How tame is too tame?" inquired *Automobile*. "Can a sports car become too good to be fun? Some of our motor-writing colleagues feel the Carrera 4 has gone too far, since it denies hero drivers the opportunity to flirt with incipient spins."

But given time to savor the Carrera 4, to reflect upon its abilities, the verdict is different.

"All-wheel drive dulls the sharper reactivity of the 911,"*Automobile* recognized, "but on balance, what's been lost is precisely what had to go. . . . If it feels less thrilling on the limit than a 911, just remember that that car could thrill you to death." Said *Auto Week*: "Some mutter about a loss of character, whine about being unable to toss the tail about . . . As for us, we've opened a door in the present, sat down in the past and driven into the future. We're going to like it there."

Perhaps the highest praise of all for Porsche's *wunderbar* wondercar comes from *Car*, the British journal notoriously critical of German machinery. The Carrera 4, says *Car*, is "the best supercar money can buy."

## *Porsche 911 Carrera 4 Major Specifications*

**Manufacturer:**

Dr. Ing. h.c. F. Porsche AG; Stuttgart, West Germany

**Dimensions:**

| | |
|---|---|
| Wheelbase, in. | 89.5 |
| Overall length, in. | 167.3 |
| Overall width, in. | 65.0 |
| Overall height, in. | 52.0 |
| Track (front), in. | 54.3 |
| Track (rear), in. | 54.1 |
| Curb weight, lbs. | 3197 |

**Powertrain:**

| | |
|---|---|
| Layout: | rear-engine, all-wheel drive |
| Engine type: | single-overhead-cam, horizontally opposed 6-cylinder |
| Displacement, liters/cubic inches | 3.6/219 |
| Horsepower @ rpm | 247 @ 6100 |
| Torque (lbs./ft.) @ rpm | 228 @ 4800 |
| Fuel delivery: | DME port fuel injection |
| Transmission: | 5-speed manual |

**Performance:**

| | |
|---|---|
| Top speed, mph | 162 |
| 0-60 mph, seconds | 5.3 |
| Quarter-mile, seconds | 13.6 |

| | |
|---|---|
| **Approximate price:** | $69,500 |

# PORSCHE
# 928 S4

I
n 1989, Porsche's most modern shape was that of the 928. Oddly, that had also been true a decade *earlier*, in 1979. Powered by a V-8 engine, it was (and continues to be) a bulbous, solidly engineered, and amazingly resourceful front-engine 2+2. Fast when launched in 1977, and even faster by the late 1980s, the 928 has always been an enigma. Here is a car whose engineering is admired by every rival, whose chassis capabilities are never in doubt. Yet it's never even *threatened* to outsell the old air-cooled 911.

The first front-engine road car worthy of the Porsche crest, the 928, roared onto the streets in 1977. Mature, respected, and fast, it nonetheless lacked the elan of the spirited 911. Porsche kept the 928 faith, however, refining it year after year, until arriving at the 928 S4 (**both pages**). It impresses the knowledgeable by offering supercar performance without exotic-car temperament.

The latest 928 edition couples a refined appearance with vicious power—a car that's not so easy to handle at the limit without a fair amount of practice. At speeds beyond 4000 rpm or so, it likes to take off like a jackrabbit on his way to a romantic interlude. In short: brute speed. But that's not been quite enough to entice the shoppers to open their checkbook.

Two factors hit Porsche very hard in 1988. One was the short-lived worldwide stock market crash, which destroyed confidence among the people who habitually bought supercars. The other negative development was that the value of the West German currency, relative to the American dollar, rose rapidly.

The result? Porsche sales in the U.S. plummeted. A great car like the 928 had to fight for its life, especially since the current edition didn't look any more modern than when introduced back in the '70s. Porsche, however, gritted its collective teeth and got on with the job it knew best: building better, and yet better, versions of a design intended to remain on the market for a long time.

The 928 saga began in the early 1970s, when Porsche decided that the 911 had to be displaced by an entirely different type of car. How wrong that judgment proved to be! More than a quarter-million 911s had been built by the late 1980s, and there was no evidence at all that sales might be drying up. (As usual, the designation 928 was a design-office project title, with no other significance.)

The 928 was everything that the 911 was not: front instead of rear engine, water-cooled instead of air, V-8 instead of a flat-six. It still ran via rear-wheel drive, though with the gearbox/final drive unit in one assembly. That's not all. It was given a sleek, but anonymous, 2+2 coupe style without any alternatives—no convertible, nor even a "Targa" option. A 928 was not a roomy car, either. The rear could best be described as a "+2" compartment, while luggage space qualified as minimal at best.

On the other hand, it sat on an excellent chassis and powertrain. Porsche had suffered years of complaints about the handling of its tail-happy 911s, so the German automaker spent more years developing a new independent suspension for the 928 that would (it hoped) take care of everything. Because the car's engineering controlled rear-wheel geometry very carefully indeed, a driver no longer had to worry about lifting a heavy foot off the throttle in mid-corner, and handling became quite exemplary.

By comparison with the 911, though, the 928 was an efficient machine that lacked soul. Porsche enthusiast Denis Jenkinson once wrote that the 911 greeted a new driver with the impression that "If you don't pay attention to your driving, I will hit back." In contrast, the 928 merely said "Leave this all to me, I'm much more capable than you are."

And so it was. In all but one respect, the 928 was a paragon of the way a fast, front-engine car should behave. It combined impressive balance with great traction, superb power-assisted steering, and a supple ride. That one trouble spot: an ample earful of road noise, which tended to spoil the otherwise restful nature of the 928's chassis. This car was much more of a Grand Tourer than the 911 could ever hope to be; so a flaw of such an ironic nature proved difficult for some customers to accept.

The original 928 of 1977 had been fast, yes, but not *really* swift. Top speed was "only" 140 mph, and the chassis felt as if it could cope with much more. The engine had only a single overhead camshaft per cylinder head. Porsche had always intended its new V-8 to have a great deal of potential, as well as a long life. So from 1979 the 928S came on the scene, with an enlarged (285-cubic inch) engine churning out 300 horsepower. Top speed rose to 150 mph. Now that was more like it.

Further improvements arrived as the car became 928 S2 in 1983, but sales continued at a leisurely 4500 units per year. Not until 1986 was the completely-developed 928 S4 ready for accolades. (There never was a Series 3 edition.) Porsche, it seemed, had gone right through the design from head to tail, liked most of what they found, yet revamped everything from the engine to the styling.

*Subtly altered tail and nose trim identifies the current 928 (**top and opposite page, bottom**), but there's nothing low key about its magnificent 5-liter double-overhead cam, 32-valve aluminum V-8 (**right**). The 316-horsepower projectile propels the 3500-pound car to 60 mph in 5.7 seconds and to a top speed of 168 mph.*

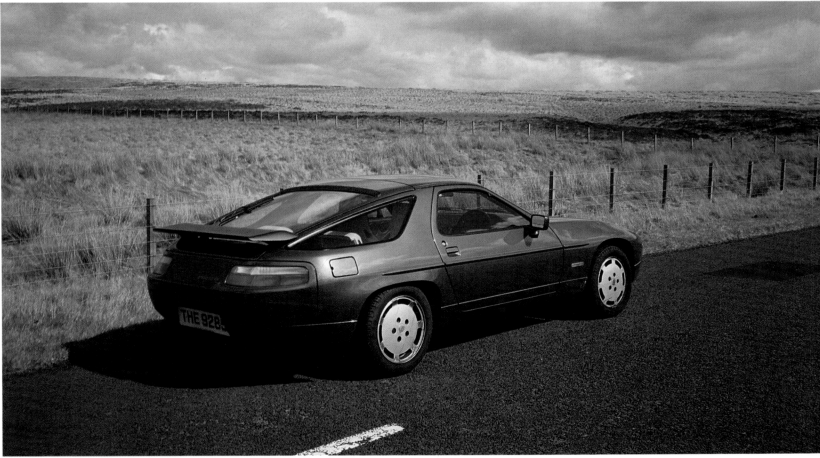

228

The most important change took place at the engine, where cars for all markets were given 4-valve cylinder heads and twin overhead camshafts, a layout already applied to U.S.-market cars. In America these cars rate 292 horsepower, but in more powerful "European" tune the 302 cubic-inch (4,957 cc) unit produces no less than 320 horsepower.

The body style, though still recognizably derived from the original bug-eyed creation of 1977, has differently detailed nose and tail sections, along with a new type of rear aerofoil. More significantly, small electric motors controlled by the engine water temperature open and close the nose cooling ducts. Sill extensions and extra front underbody panels help to smooth the car's aerodynamics.

Porsche was proud to claim a new, low drag coefficient of 0.34 for the S4; but ashamed to admit that the old car had been encumbered with a distinctly average figure of 0.39.

Even in the late 1980s the 928, in S4 form, still has image problems. It is now a very fast car, with 160-mph top speed and the ability to rush up to 100 mph in no more than 15 seconds. The old-fashioned 911 Turbo, on the other hand, is quicker, no less fuel-efficient, and still a strong seller. Porsche, thank goodness, has always seen the 911 and the 928 as selling to different people. So the company has been happy to go on building both types.

*According to one road tester, the credo of the raucous rear-engine 911 is, "If you don't pay attention to your driving, I will hit back." The 928 says, "Leave this all to me, I'm much more capable than you are." Pop-up bug-eye headlamps (**left**) and unabashedly rounded styling polarize opinion on the 928 S4's looks.*

## Porsche 928 S4 Major Specifications

**Manufacturer:**

Dr. Ing. h.c. F. Porsche AG; Stuttgart, West Germany

**Dimensions:**

| | |
|---|---|
| Wheelbase, in. | 98.4 |
| Overall length, in. | 178.1 |
| Overall width, in. | 72.3 |
| Overall height, in. | 50.5 |
| Track (front), in. | 61.1 |
| Track (rear), in. | 60.9 |
| Curb weight, lbs. | 3505 |

**Powertrain:**

| | |
|---|---|
| Layout: | front-engine, rear-wheel drive |
| Engine Type: | double overhead-cam V-8 |
| Displacement, liters/cubic inches | 5.0/302.5 |
| Horsepower @ rpm | 316 @ 6000 |
| Torque (lbs./ft.) @ rpm | 317 @ 3000 |
| Fuel delivery: | LH-Jetronic port fuel injection |
| Transmission: | 5-speed manual or 4-speed automatic |

**Performance:**

| | |
|---|---|
| Top speed, mph | 168 |
| 0-60 mph, seconds | 5.7 |
| Quarter-mile, seconds | 14.1 |

| | |
|---|---|
| **Approximate price:** | $74,545 |

229

232

significant suspension and brake upgrades, and, just for good measure, a larger turbocharger that delivered an additional 30 horsepower. Trouble was, only 700 of the Turbo S models were imported in 1988, and they carried a premium of more than $7000 over the already hefty price of a 944. That made the $48,000 944 Turbo S one of the world's most expensive 4-cylinder cars. Porsche's performance consciousness told it that the Turbo S package was a good thing. But the October 1987 stock market plunge had thrown a scare into Porsche's clientele, and sales were down. To its credit, Porsche took steps in 1989 to reconcile two forces that are usually opposed: higher performance and lower price.

First, it decided that all 944 Turbos should be of the S persuasion; the package was no longer an option, and the S designation was dropped. Secondly, in April of '89, the company actually reduced the price of the 944 line. The 944 Turbo started the model year listing for $47,600 and finished it at $44,900. Okay, $45,000 is still a chunk of change, but the 944 Turbo is a hunk of machine.

Try a top speed of 162 mph. That's supercar territory. Zero to 60 mph is down to 5.7 seconds and the quarter-mile passes in just 14.1. Spectacular, yes, but some critics nonetheless argue that the base 1989 944 S2 is actually a better car for day to day use. That's because its 16-valve 3-liter four is naturally aspirated and can deliver its 211 horsepower and 206 pounds/feet of torque sans turbo lag. Without the Turbo car's larger front disc brakes, larger tires, and beefier suspension pieces, the S2 is also about 66 pounds lighter than its more powerful brother. Lighter weight and more immediate throttle response help the S2 feel somewhat more responsive around town and coming out of corners. But the difference here is the one between quickness and speed. The 944 S2 runs to 60 mph in 6.9 seconds and runs out of

The level of refinement built into the 944 Turbo (**both pages**) takes some supercar fans by surprise. **Car and Driver** tested a 944 Turbo-spec Porsche and found that, "despite the car's prodigious horsepower and high braking and cornering limits, it doesn't feel like a high-strung boy racer. It's remarkably forgiving, and you never have to guess its next move. . . . You'll have a hard time finding a GT machine as easy to drive fast and as easy to live with . . . ."

233

944 Turbo uses pop-up headlamps and integrated driving lights (**opposite page, top left**). Its all-aluminum, single overhead-cam engine (**opposite page, bottom**) makes it, according to **Car and Driver**, "by far the strongest-performing 4-cylinder car in the world." The lucky driver is greeted by clear, analog instrumentation and an air bag in the steering-wheel hub (**top**), while the leather-covered front sport bucket seats tilt for access to token rear jump seats (**above**).

steam at 149 mph. For all-out *Autobahn* burning, then, it's clear that the Turbo is the way to go, and Porsche equips the 944 Turbo for just such duty.

Like the S2, the Turbo's transaxle is located at the rear, for a virtual 50-50 weight distribution. But the Turbo's 5-speed manual transmission gets an external oil cooler and a limited slip differential. The S2's quickness is enhanced by a 3.875 final-drive ratio, while the Turbo's legs are extended by a 3.375 final ratio. Both cars have a four piston, fixed-caliper, power-assisted anti-lock braking system, but the Turbo's vented front discs are larger. The Turbo's chassis is built to accommodate its increased horsepower, with firmer springs and shock absorbers, and a thicker stabilizer bar and more rigid suspension bushings for precise and responsive handling. It comes with forged alloy wheels in the "club sport" design. They're seven inches wide in front and nine inches wide the rear. Ultra high-performance tires measure 225/50ZR16 in front and 245/50ZR16 in the rear. In addition to the standard appointments found on the 944 S2, the 944 Turbo comes with a stereo system that includes 10 speakers and a four-channel, 100-watt amplifier. Safety is enhanced by air bags for both the driver and passenger.

*Car and Driver* tested a 944 Turbo-spec Porsche and found that, "despite the car's prodigious horsepower and high braking and cornering limits, it doesn't feel like a high-strung boy racer. It's remarkably forgiving, and you never have to guess its next move. All the information you need to stay on the road and in control is faithfully telegraphed to your palms and the seat of your pants."

Inside, the clear, analog instrumentation and the placement of controls is up to the car's performance potential. "It offers no distractions from the business at hand, which is driving hard and fast," the magazine said. "The seats are supportive, the pedals are ideally placed for heel and toe tap dancing, the shifter sides into gear by telepathy . . . . "

"You'll have a hard time finding a GT machine as easy to drive fast and as easy to live with . . . " *Car and Driver* concluded. "It's by far the strongest-performing 4-cylinder car in the world, and only a few cars of any stripe can match or beat its numbers. The same holds true for its combination of mechanical smoothness, creature comforts, and handling precision."

Porsche may not play by the numbers, but the numbers it plays with usually turn up winners. And so it is with the 944 Turbo.

## Porsche 944 Turbo Major Specifications

**Manufacturer:**

Dr. Ing. h.c. F. Porsche AG; Stuttgart, West Germany

**Dimensions:**

| | |
|---|---:|
| Wheelbase, in. | 94.5 |
| Overall length, in. | 168.9 |
| Overall width, in. | 68.3 |
| Overall height, in. | 50.2 |
| Track (front), in. | 57.4 |
| Track (rear), in. | 56.5 |
| Curb weight, lbs. | 2998 |

**Powertrain:**

| | |
|---|---:|
| Layout: | front-engine, rear-wheel drive |
| Engine type: | turbocharged, single-overhead-cam inline 4-cylinder |
| Displacement, liters/cubic inches | 2.5/151 |
| Horsepower @ rpm | 247 @ 6000 |
| Torque (lbs./ft.) @ rpm | 258 @ 4000 |
| Fuel delivery: | DME port fuel injection |
| Transmission: | 5-speed manual |

**Performance:**

| | |
|---|---:|
| Top speed, mph | 162 |
| 0-60 mph, seconds | 5.7 |
| Quarter-mile, seconds | 14.1 |
| **Approximate price:** | $44,900 |

# PORSCHE 959

Perhaps once or twice in a generation comes a car that has no peer. One such car carries an easy-to-remember number—959—a number that's destined to go down in auto history with no further explanation needed. When the 959 went on sale in 1985 that number was, quite simply, the designation for the fastest, the most complex, and the most expensive Porsche ever made. In short, the champ.

As *Automobile* magazine described it in 1987, the 959 is "a car that rewrites all the rules" and "nudges the performance realms of today's racing cars." Even more surprising, it is a vehicle "that any man or woman with average experience can master ... within a short learning period." We're talking about a car that packs 450 horsepower behind it, uses six forward speeds and 4-wheel-drive to unleash all that brute force, and can hit 60 mph not in 5 or 6 seconds, but in about 3.7 seconds. Porsche's 959 can race to a hundred in less time than it takes an ordinary above-average performer to reach 60!

The 959 is a car conceived with motorsport in mind, but frustrated by a change of rules. All Porsche enthusiasts, however, give thanks

With the exuberant, ultra-capable 959 (**both pages**), Porsche has achieved not only the crowning glory of one of the automotive age's most enduring designs, but it just may be pointing the way to the sports car of the 21st Century. The 959 remembers its roots as a rear-engine 911, but fashions from them its own, all-wheel-drive, 190-mph identity. Production ran to just 200 959s.

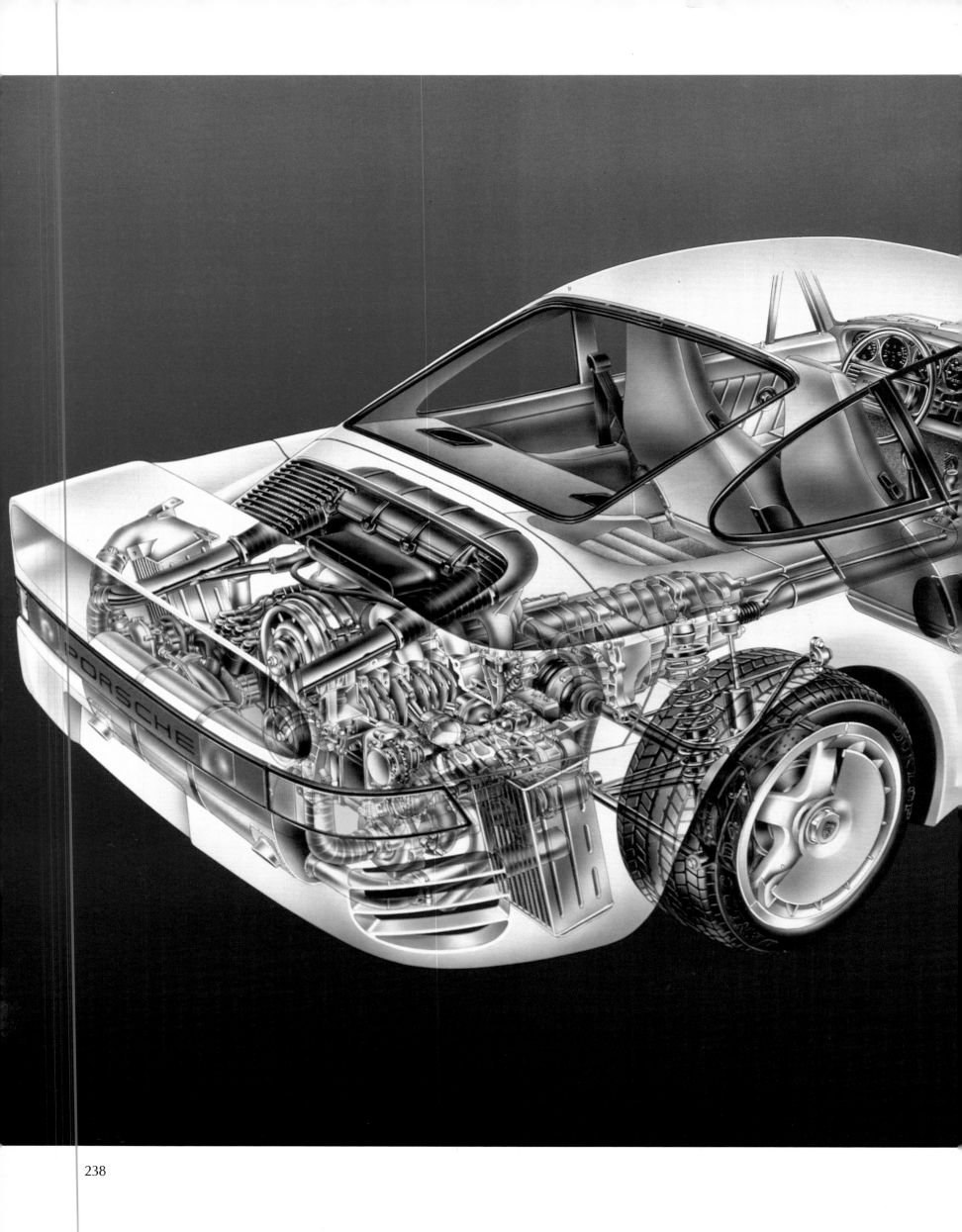

that the West German company persevered with development of its first 4-wheel drive car, and eventually marketed the result.

Once Porsche's engineers decide to tackle a particular project, they always make a thorough job of it. This explains why the 959 was conceived early in the 1980s, first shown as a motorsport-oriented design study in 1983, nominally promised for first deliveries in 1985—but didn't actually go on sale (in tiny numbers) until the end of 1987.

The 959's protracted genesis can be explained by Porsche's renowned urge to get rid of all possible failings before releasing any car to the public. Along the way, in those tedious years when its very existence appeared to be a mirage, the 959 evolved from an out-and-out competition machine into a meticulously developed and environmentally acceptable road car. Professor Helmut Bott, head of Porsche development, explained that "the 959 was neither a rallye nor off-road car in the basic concept." Instead, the company "wanted to build a competitive car in the prescribed series of 200 which would be suitable for road use without major changes."

One thing did not change. Porsche always said it would build only 200 examples, and that aim was never revised.

The roots of the 959 lie in the famous rear-engine 911. In reality, though, the production 959 retains very few links with the 911, apart from a generally similar profile, a few body panels, and the use of a flat-six engine mounted in the extreme tail.

One basic difference is that the 911 has an air-cooled flat-six engine driving the rear wheels. The 959 puts water-cooled cylinder heads on the same basic engine, but also adds a very sophisticated 4-wheel-drive installation.

The original 959 prototype featured a much-modified 911 monocoque structure in which a simple 4-wheel-drive "conversion" had been installed. "Works" competition cars built to run the 1984 Paris-Dakar rally, across the Sahara Desert, were simple 911 conversions. This was good enough to win, but for 1985 and '86 more representative 959 prototypes were entered in the same event—and won once again!

The engine is a developed version of the one originally used in the 956 and 962 2-seater racing Porsches. It features a curious mixture

*The original 959 prototype featured a much-modified 911 monocoque structure in which a simple four-wheel-drive "conversion" had been installed. The production 959 (left) is much more sophisticated. This view exposes its all-independent suspension, its 6-speed main gearbox, the hardware for its variable front-to-rear torque split, and its limited-slip differentials.*

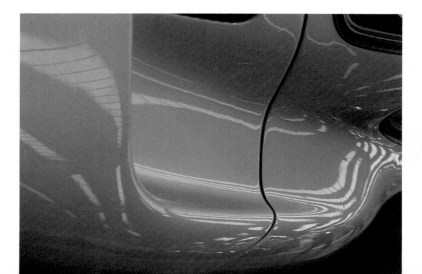

Before deliveries began, the 959 was gradually and persistently developed away from its motorsport layout. Thus, the definitive production cars are luxuriously finished, to justify the asking price. Basic cabin dimensions and proportions are the same as other members of the 911 family, though the wheel tracks are much wider and fenders correspondingly more bulbous. It also has engine bay air intakes behind the doors and wide "running boards" along the sides, under the door cutouts.

Compared with the 911, the 959 has a smoother nose, with fully integrated bumpers. A wrap-over but completely functional rear spoiler stands above the engine deck. The net result is a drag coefficient as low as 0.32.

No one expected such a car to be cheap, but there was never any shortage of customers for what was very likely the world's fastest road car of the day. Nor was it all wasted effort on Porsche's behalf. Many of the lessons of the 959 were later incorporated into the new-for-1989 Carrera 4, which also has 4-wheel-drive but a much more affordable price tag.

The 959's flat six (**opposite page top and lower left**) is a developed version of that used in the 956 and 962 racing Porsches. Its cylinder heads are cooled by water, while the cylinder barrels are cooled by air. Twin intercooled KKK turbochargers working in series extract 450 horsepower from 174 cubic inches. The 959's lines pave the way for a generation of Porsches to come. Its wheel design has already be imitated by other manufacturers, though no rival has chanced yet to copy the integrated style of the 959's headlamps. Neither has any captured the sculpted grace of the air intake on the 959's rear fender (**opposite page, bottom right**).

of water cooling for the cylinder heads and traditional-style air cooling for the cylinder barrels. To extract the vast 450 horsepower output from a 174-cubic inch (2850 cc) engine demands a pair of KKK turbochargers and twin intercoolers. Unlike other such cars, the turbos work in series (one blowing into the other), not in parallel. This means one turbo is always working strongly from low engine revs, the other chiming in at full throttle, and at high engine rpm.

Such is this magnificent race-proved engine's efficiency that even with a maximum turbo boost of 14.4 psi, running on nothing stronger than 95-octane fuel, it still produces 2.6 horsepower per cubic inch. For competition use, the engine can be tuned to deliver between 650 and 700 horsepower, while maintaining the sort of long-term reliability for which Porsches are noted.

The real charm of the 959, however, lies not in its sheer acceleration (which is phenomenal enough), but in its ultra-sophisticated 4-wheel-drive system. That unit features a 6-speed main gearbox, along with electronic monitoring and control of limited-slip differentials in the drive line. With the aid of fat tires, an anti-lock braking system (ABS) and power-assisted steering, the 959's cornering power, traction, and general stability and security can probably best those of any other car of the same period.

More importantly, here is the first Porsche that doesn't have to be driven delicately on wet or slippery roads, nor steered carefully around tight wet corners. With its variable front-to-rear torque split, electronic controls, and amazingly grippy chassis, this is a full-fledged supercar.

Yes, the 959 is a truly rapid machine. Porsche has been reluctant to claim a high maximum speed, but independent tests put this figure at more than 195 mph. Besides that, the car is utterly docile in traffic, can be driven equally hard on the *Autobahn* or in the mountains, and displays the sort of Teutonic attention to detail that promises a long and exciting life.

When *Road & Track* tested nine of the world's fastest cars in 1987, they ran a pair of 959s: a well-equipped Deluxe and a stripped-down Sport. The slowpoke took all of 4 seconds to reach 60 mph, and could squeeze out only a 197-mph top speed. The lighter-weight Sport edition knocked that 0-60 time down to 3.6, and hit 100 in 8.2 seconds (versus 9.4 for the Deluxe); but managed only one extra mile per hour at the top end. "Everything comes so easily to the car," said Phil Hill after pushing one of those 959s to its limit. "More than any of the others, it feels like a normal car speeding along the highway, even at these high speeds."

## Porsche 959 Major Specifications

**Manufacturer:**

Dr. Ing. h.c. F. Porsche AG; Stuttgart, West Germany

**Dimensions:**

| | |
|---|---|
| Wheelbase, in. | 89.4 |
| Overall length, in. | 167.7 |
| Overall width, in. | 72.4 |
| Overall height, in. | 47.2 |
| Track (front), in. | 59.2 |
| Track (rear), in. | 61.0 |
| Curb weight, lbs. | 2977 (Deluxe 3190) |

**Powertrain:**

| | |
|---|---|
| Layout: | rear-engine, four-wheel drive |
| Engine type: | twin turbocharged, double-overhead-cam, horizontally opposed 6-cylinder |
| Displacement, liters/cubic inches | 2.8/174 |
| Horsepower (DIN) @ rpm | 450 @ 6500 |
| Torque (lbs./ft.) @ rpm | 369 @ 5500 |
| Fuel delivery: | Bosch Motronic fuel injection |
| Transmission: | 6-speed manual |

**Performance:**

| | |
|---|---|
| Top speed, mph | 193-plus |
| 0-60 mph, seconds | 3.7 |
| Quarter-mile, seconds | est. 11.9 |

| | |
|---|---|
| **Approximate price:** | $230,000 (1987) |

# PORSCHE 962

Porsche's tally of 16 Daytona 24-Hour and 12 Le Mans wins dating back to 1970 is a formidable record likely never to be duplicated—only expanded, as Porsche continues to rack up victories. Zuffenhausen's winningest is a five-year-old design, the Type 962. It has proved itself so convincingly in competition that the 962, in terms of overall accomplishment, remains *the* premiere racing machine of all time.

In the world of top-level racing cars, there are cars and there are legends. Only a very few make it to the legend category, and they come easily to mind. Bugatti, with its string of wins in the late '20s, is another. Bentley and Alfa-Romeo dominated endurance racing for several years running. Then BMW and Mercedes-Benz, the prewar giants, gave European sports car and Grand Prix racing a decidedly

Porsche began its unmatched era of racing dominance in the late 1960s. It took its first World Manufacturer's Championship in 1969, and is still going strong two decades later. A key to its success is the Type 962 (**both pages**). The mid-engine marauder has proved itself so convincingly that in terms of overall accomplishment, it's probably the premier racing machine of all time.

244

German flavor. After World War II, Mercedes-Benz again dominated long-distance racing. The Italians burst back on the scene with Ferrari's immortal decade of victories. Then Ford captured the limelight with a long session of dominance, which ended when Porsche rose to the occasion with the tubular-frame Types 908 and 917.

Those cars of the late '60s began an unmatched era of dominance. Porsche took its first World Manufacturer's Championship in 1969 and hasn't quit 20 years later. Other marques dented Porsche's armor from time to time, but overall, the German autocrafters have built a racing reputation equaled by none. Their tally of victories is testimony to the marque's extraordinary breeding.

Porsche 917s took two consecutive World Endurance Championship titles in 1970 and '71, while nailing down endurance wins in the 24-hour races at both Le Mans and Daytona. Daytona wins in 1973 and '75, along with a succession of six straight victories from 1977 through '83 with the turbocharged Type 935, were complemented by five Le Mans triumphs through 1982 with Type 936 and 956 Porsches.

In America, the fledgling International Motor Sport Association of 1969 grew into a professional and amateur series with 61 season races in 1982. From 1971 onward, Porsche has received championship laurels in one or more IMSA categories every year except one (1984). In all 561 IMSA races through 1985, Porsches won 233, an unbelievable 42 percent.

The Jim Busby-owned Miller Porsche team found the winning combination at the 1989 24-Hours of Daytona (**opposite page, top row**). Team members included Derek Bell, Bob Welleck, and John Andretti. The heart of the 962 is the exceedingly well-developed double-overhead-cam, 3-liter, air-cooled flat six (**bottom left**). The turbocharged and injected engine develops 600 horsepower at 7800 rpm. Like all 962s, Dyson Racing's car (**bottom right**) has an aluminum monocoque chassis. It weighs in at a race-ready 2070 pounds.

By the early '80s, the 935 had been superseded by the new GTPrototype cars, beginning with Brian Redman's Lola-Chevrolet championship car of 1981. Porsche factory engineers used their four-time Le Mans winning Type 956 as a guide and produced the 962, which was unveiled for competition at Daytona in 1984.

Weighing in at 2070 pounds, the 962 dices through turns and churns down straights at more than 225 mph. Power for the car, being very similar to the 956, comes from Porsche's ancient but exceedingly well-developed double-overhead-cam, 3.0-liter (183 cubic-inch), air-cooled "boxer" 6-cylinder. Resting in an aluminum monocoque chassis, the 2-valve-per-cylinder, dry-sump lubricated engine cranks out 600 horsepower at 7800 rpm. Torque of 510 pounds/feet peaks at 5900 rpm. High-octane racing fuel is metered by Bosch Motronic fuel injection and stuffed into cylinders by a single KKK turbocharger with dual wastegates. A Bosch electronic ignition fires the mixture in hemispherical combustion chambers with a 7.0:1 compression ratio. Exhaust gases leave the back of the car and greet the world with four-foot-long flames when the driver backs off on the pedal.

Porsche's equally proven 5-speed all-synchromesh transaxle delivers power through a Sachs single-plate competition clutch and a locked differential. Rear wheels are suspended by unequal-length A-arms and titanium coil springs, dampened by coil-over Bilstein gas-filled shock absorbers. The front suspension, again conventional Porsche, also consists of unequal-length A-arms, coil springs, and shocks; but with a twin-blade anti-sway bar rather than the single blade used in the rear. BBS 16-inch diameter wheels, 13 inches wide in the front and 14.5 inches aft, scrub off speed through 13-inch ventilated outboard-mounted disc brakes with dual calipers per disc. A 31.7-gallon (120-liter) fuel tank with a 5-liter reserve gives a racing range of around 130 miles.

Like many previous Porsches, the Type 962 quickly became a winner. Since its debut at Daytona, the cars have won 50 of IMSA's 79 Camel GT races for a phenomenal 63-percent win record. Following the 1985 Porsche 962 1-2-3 blitz at Daytona, they've won every year, except for a 1988 upset pulled off by Jaguar. Add to these wins the back-to-back 1986 and '87 Le Mans victories by the 962's Group C counterpart, the 962C, and the result is legendary status on the race course.

Camel GT driver Steve Millen told *Road & Track* in 1987 that even though there is "nothing exceptional about the 962....the Porsche is a super car to drive for 24 hours because it's a complete package. It's been around so long and has been refined, modified and made so reliable that it's just bulletproof."

In addition to Daytona, Jaguar won the Le Mans enduro in 1988 as well as the international Sports Prototype crown. Porsche edged out the British make in the IMSA series, however. A year earlier, the 962 Porsche won every IMSA race except one that was taken by Nissan and two won by Jaguar. The 962 led 305 points to Chevrolet's 79 in second spot. The 1988 results reflect a strange twist of fate: With only three wins to Nissan's nine, Porsche was favored in the point tally because of so many high 962 finishes, and earned its fifth consecutive IMSA Camel GT manufacturer's championship.

Whether in the hands of Bayside Motorsport (six wins in eleven races during 1987), Holbert Racing (Chip Robinson taking the IMSA title that year with four wins and three seconds), or the Bob Dyson Racing team (three wins), the 962s were formidable in 1987. Of course, a dozen or so different 962s were participating in the Camel GT circuit in the mid-1980s, so they had more than a few opportunities. The 1988 campaign was somewhat different, as the 962 faced increased competition from Nissan and Jaguar.

It was the late Al Holbert, team owner, five-time IMSA champion and all-time IMSA leading driver, who led the way in 962 development. By 1987, his Lowenbrau Special 962 Porsches reached 720 horsepower at 7800 rpm. Working closely with Andial of Santa Ana, California, Holbert and all Porsche teams using Andial engines made GTP racing a tough business. Now that Holbert is gone and the Porsche factory has dropped development of both its 962 and 956 lines, no longer competing as a factory, the great age of the Porsche 962 moves into the hands of privateers like Andial.

The main goal of the firm is to adapt the water-cooled 956 twin turbocharged flat-6 engine in place of its air-cooled forbearer. Andial's engine chief, Alwin Springer, says the conversion will be made competitive. Unavoidably, though, the Porsches have edged into the underdog "old race car" category against the latest generation of GTP machines.

Thinking of the now-legendary Porsche 962 as an underdog is the sort of irony that befalls many great faltering champions. New adversaries measure their performance against the champ, then hone their talents to beat him. But as shown by the winning Jim Busby-owned Miller Porsche team at the 1989 running of the 24-Hours of Daytona, the 962 isn't over the hill yet.

*The cockpit of Jim Busby's Miller Porsche 962 (opposite page, top) brims with all the gauges and controls necessary for a 24-Hours of Daytona win. The 5-speed gearshift lever is to the right of the driver's seat. A KKK turbocharger sits prominently atop the flat six (opposite page, bottom). A Dyson Racing 962 (above) shows the aerodynamic aids that help it run at 200 mph.*

## Porsche 962 Major Specifications

**Manufacturer:**

Dr. Ing. h.c. F. Porsche AG; Stuttgart, West Germany
Holbert Racing; U.S.A.

**Dimensions:**

| | |
|---|---|
| Wheelbase, in. | 104.0 |
| Overall length, in. | 188.0 |
| Overall width, in. | 78.0 |
| Overall height, in. | 41.0 |
| Track (front), in. | 65.0 |
| Track (rear), in. | 61.0 |
| Curb weight, lbs. | 2100 |

**Powertrain:**

| | |
|---|---|
| Layout: | mid-engine, rear-wheel drive |
| Engine type: | turbocharged single-overhead-cam, horizontally opposed 6-cylinder |
| Displacement, liters/cubic inches | 3.0/183 |
| Horsepower @ rpm | 680/720 @ 7800 |
| Torque (lbs./ft.) @ rpm | 530 @ 5700 |
| Fuel delivery: | Bosch Motronic fuel injection |
| Transmission: | 5-speed manual |

**Performance:**

| | |
|---|---|
| Top speed, mph | 240 |
| 0-60 mph, seconds | NA |
| Quarter-mile, seconds | NA |
| | |
| Approximate price: | $380,000 |

# RUF TWIN-TURBO PORSCHE

Alois Ruf does Porsches only one way, the right way, from impeccably turned out wheels (**bottom left**) to subtle bodywork modifications that blend function and fashion. His dedication to excellence holds in the engine bay, where the Ruf touch turns the 911 Turbo's already potent flat six into an omnipotent force that bequeaths 469 horsepower on the driver fortunate enough to acquire it (**right**). His 211-mph Yellow Bird (**below and bottom right pages**) reigned supreme in a high-speed shoot out among nine supercars.

Competing against eight of the fastest cars in the world in 1987 at Volkswagen's German test track, a Ruf "Yellow Bird" reached a speed of 211 mph—some 10 mph faster than its nearest rival. "The engine sounds absolutely magnificent and the power is amazing," reported former Le Mans winner Paul Frere in *Road & Track*. Phil Hill added that "The Yellow Bird is just steady as a rock at over 200 mph."

Phenomenal top speed is only part of the Ruf story, though. Add 0-60 mph acceleration in a staggering 4 seconds, plus 11.7 seconds through the quarter-mile, and this is one fast Bavarian machine.

Only a handful of Twin-Turbos have been built. As the company itself admits, "for most people, owning a Ruf car will remain a dream. Only a very select few will ever experience the speed, power, performance and excellence of ride."

All this magic takes place in the Ruf Automobiles shop in the small town of Pfaffenhausen, located in scenic Bavaria near the King Ludwig castles. Run today by Alois Ruf (pronounced Luis Roof), son of the founder of a service station, Ruf & Co. molds Porsche's 911 into one of the world's fastest cars. Each member of the service group is a specialist, whether in body modification; engine assembly, repair or tuning; chassis tuning; paint; cockpit design; or electronic systems. Each car is built to customer specifications, but always starting with a Porsche 911. Single-turbo adaptations were built first, followed more recently by the Twin.

When complete, the transformation of what was previously known as the Porsche 930 is the Ruf Turbo. As is the case with other specialty autocrafters, the Ruf name attached to the finished product raises a serious question: Is the car still a Porsche? It certainly *looks* like a Porsche. The big difference is that the basic Porsche ingredients have

now entered the 200-mph realm, all in a fully certified automobile. These are not gray-market cars but highly refined and expensive machines for the connoisseur of "ultimate" automobiles, as defined by Ruf.

The latest Ruf turbo begins with a basic 911 Carrera shell and becomes the Ruf Twin-Turbo. A separate turbocharger and intercooler supply each bank of cylinders. Engine management stems from a pressure-sensitive electronic control system, developed in collaboration with the Robert Bosch Company. The result is largely maintenance-free operation. No ignition or fuel adjustments are necessary.

Is the Ruf Twin-Turbo a rival to Porsche's own 911 Turbo? Perhaps the little shop in Bavaria goes a bit beyond what Stuttgart had in mind, but the difference is dramatic, especially in dollars. The 911 Turbo already sits in the economic stratosphere at over $71,000, and reaches 0-60 mph in 5.1 seconds. Quarter-mile times of 13.6 seconds are a full half-second quicker than a European-tuned Ferrari GTO. And the Italian costs a bundle more.

What does the Ruf Twin-Turbo do? Quite simply, for $150,000-plus it delivers the quickest 0-60 mph and quarter-mile times available in a production automobile today. That's what Alois Ruf is all about.

The small staff of around 25 craftsmen at Ruf Automobiles construct specialty cars in small numbers for an exclusive clientele. A 911 shell is assembled to order with a slope nose (Porsche 935 configuration) or standard Porsche sheet metal. Customers have a choice of wide or narrow track, fender flares or plain, with or without a huge whale tail, along with lots of other Porsche hardware and/or Ruf pieces. All this is available to a couple of dozen discriminating buyers each year, all of whom are handpicked by Ruf himself. He won't sell his cars to

just anyone. If an owner of a 911 wants his Porsche updated by Ruf, that can also be arranged—but again at Ruf's discretion. The Ruf staff does new-car assembly and old-car restoration, and will be expanding when the company's new facilities are complete.

The Ruf name is, after all, rather new. Still, most great success stories seem to start small. In 1984, when *Road & Track* magazine staged its shootout to find Europe's fastest car, the Ruf name exploded on the international scene with a winning 186.2 mph. More came later.

*Road & Track's* competition included only manufacturers, so in the judgment of the German government, Ruf Automobiles is a manufacturer, not a tuner or restorer. Like Porsche, BMW, and Volkswagen, each Ruf automobile carries its own identification plate and serial number. The particular car used in the *Road & Track* test was, in fact, a customer's car—borrowed from Ruf's attorney for the occasion. With thousands of kilometers already on the car's odometer, winning the shootout was especially significant. What was the competition? Just 17 of the most exclusive cars in the world, including a Ferrari Boxer 512i, a Porsche 928S and 911 Turbo, and an Aston Martin Vantage. Quite a heady collection.

Each basic 911 modified by Ruf receives a Ruf-designed 5-speed transaxle built in Pfaffenhausen from Getrag pieces. Ruf-designed spoilers accent the exterior. Close attention is applied to oil coolers, huge intercoolers, four-pipe stainless steel exhaust systems, Mahle manufactured pistons (to Ruf specifications), plus special cylinders and camshafts to create an engine rated at 374 horsepower. Add to that auspicious beginning a thorough suspension tuning with Ruf parts: anti-sway bars, torsion bars, bigger brakes, Ruf-designed wheels,

special high-performance tires (once strictly Yokohama, but now Dunlop), and various other extras.

The engine of a Ruf Turbo begins as an air-cooled flat-six from Porsche's 911 lineage. It's a 930 series punched out by one millimeter to a 98.0-mm bore, with a 7:1 compression ratio. Displacement grows from 3.3 liters to 3.37 (called the 3.4-liter). Then the specialty equipment begins. New larger-fin cylinder barrels improve thermal efficiency, while bigger valve heads boost volumetric efficiency. Hotter camshafts and a higher-performance manifold along with improved exhaust manifolds and a suitcase-size aluminum intercooler increase output from the 930 configuration's 282 horsepower to the single-turbo Ruf level: 374 horsepower at 6800 rpm. Maximum torque reaches 354 pounds/feet at 4800 rpm, giving formidable acceleration with the Ruf Turbo's 9.36:1 final drive ratio. Output of

Factory Porsche 911 Turbos made do with a 4-speed manual transmission until 1989, but for several years Ruf has been fitting his 911 Turbos with a 5-speed transaxle, built to his design from Getrag pieces (**opposite page, bottom left**). Ruf interiors are usually simple and to the point (**opposite page, bottom right**). The German Porsche wizard also offers a variety of steel body panels, including fender extensions and a spoiler (**above**) that transform the stock-looking 911 tail (**opposite page, top**).

the Twin-Turbo "Yellow Bird" stretches considerably further, reaching 469 horsepower at 5959 rpm.

When *Road & Track* resumed the challenge of finding Europe's fastest car in 1987, Ruf was there again. Once more, the creations of Alois Ruf stood among the very best automobiles. And when his Twin-Turbo flashed through the timing traps at an astounding 211 mph, he retained the distinction of maker of the "fastest." The yardstick of acceleration, 0-60 mph, was achieved in 4 seconds flat, and quarter-mile times of 11.7 seconds were recorded—all with the reliability and unfussiness that has become the measure of Ruf Automobiles.

Such achievements qualified Ruf Automobiles in 1984, and again in 1987, as the maker of the "world's fastest production car." The Ruf Twin-Turbo Porsche is one fantasy car that's no fantasy at all.

*The small staff of around 25 craftsmen at Ruf Automobiles in Germany constructs specialty cars in small numbers for an exclusive clientele. Besides extensive mechanical upgrades, the firm offers expertly crafted bodywork that mimics that of the Porsche 935 race car (both pages). Prices are steep, but money alone is no entre. Ruf handpicks only a couple of dozen discriminating clients each year. He won't sell his cars to just anyone. That's the Ruf way.*

## Ruf Twin-Turbo Porsche Major Specifications

**Manufacturer:**

Ruf Automobiles GmbH; Pfaffenhausen, West Germany

**Dimensions:**

| | |
|---|---|
| Wheelbase, in. | 89.5 |
| Overall length, in. | 168.9 |
| Overall width, in. | 66.9 |
| Overall height, in. | 51.6 |
| Track (front), in. | 55.1 |
| Track (rear), in. | 56.3 |
| Curb weight, lbs. | 2530 |

**Powertrain:**

| | |
|---|---|
| Layout: | rear-engine, rear-wheel drive |
| Engine type: | twin turbocharged, single-overhead-cam, horizontally opposed 6-cylinder |
| Displacement, liters/cubic inches | 3.4/205 |
| Horsepower (DIN) @ rpm | 469 @ 5950 |
| Torque (lbs./ft.) @ rpm | 415 @ 5100 |
| Fuel delivery: | electronic fuel injection |
| Transmission: | 5-speed manual |

**Performance:**

| | |
|---|---|
| Top speed, mph | 211 |
| 0-60 mph, seconds | 4.0 |
| Quarter-mile, seconds | 11.7 |
| **Approximate price:** | $175,000 |

# INDEX